SMART GUIDE

CREATIVE
HOMEOWNER®

garages
& carports
step-by-step projects

SILT BRANCH LIBRARY
Phone: 970-876-5500
P.O. Box 10 • 600 Home Ave.
Silt, CO 81652

CREATIVE HOMEOWNER®, Upper Saddle River, New Jersey

COPYRIGHT © 1992, 2008

CREATIVE
HOMEOWNER®

A Division of Federal Marketing Corp.
Upper Saddle River, NJ

This book may not be reproduced, either in part or in its entirety, in any form, by any means, without written permission from the publisher, with the exception of brief excerpts for purposes of radio, television, or published review. All rights, including the right of translation, are reserved. *Note:* Be sure to familiarize yourself with manufacturer's instructions for tools, equipment, and materials before beginning a project. Although all possible measures have been taken to ensure the accuracy of the material presented, neither the author nor the publisher is liable in case of misinterpretation of directions, misapplication, or typographical error.

SMARTGUIDE® and Creative Homeowner® are registered trademarks of Federal Marketing Corp.

Editor: Fran J. Donegan
Photo Researcher: Robyn Poplasky
Junior Editor: Jennifer Calvert
Editorial Assistant: Nora Grace
Digital Imaging Specialist: Frank Dyer
Graphic Designers: Maureen Mulligan, Michelle D. Halko
Illustrators: Clarke Barre, Frank Rohrbach
Cover Photography: Eric Roth
Cover Design: Maureen Mulligan, Clarke Barre

Creative Homeowner
Vice President and Publisher: Timothy O. Bakke
Production Director: Kimberly H. Vivas
Art Director: David Geer
Managing Editor: Fran J. Donegan

Current Printing (last digit)
10 9 8 7 6 5 4 3 2 1

Manufactured in the United States of America

Smart Guide: Garages & Carports
First published as *Quick Guide: Garages & Carports*
Library of Congress Control Number: 2007933889
ISBN 10: 1-58011-394-X
ISBN 13: 978-1-58011-394-6

CREATIVE HOMEOWNER®
24 Park Way
Upper Saddle River, NJ 07458
www.creativehomeowner.com

Photo Credits

page 1: courtesy of Clopay **page 3:** *top* Bill Rothschild; *center* Tony Giammarino/Giammarino & Dworkin; *bottom* Anne Gummerson **page 5:** *top right* Anne Gummerson; *bottom right* Bill Rothschild; *bottom left* Tony Giammarino/Giammarino & Dworkin; *top left* courtesy of Clopay **page 13:** *top right* Eric Roth; *bottom* Anne Gummerson; *top left* courtesy of Clopay **page 21:** *top* courtesy of Monier Life Tile; *bottom right* Eric Roth; *bottom left* George Ross/CH **page 27:** *top right & bottom* Tony Giammarino/Giammarino & Dworkin; *top left* Eric Roth **page 39:** *right & top left* Eric Roth; *bottom left* courtesy of Clopay **page 51:** *top right* Stan Sudol/CH; *bottom* courtesy of Clopay; *top left* Bill Rothschild **page 65:** *top right* Brian Vanden Brink, architect: Whitten Winkleman Architects; *bottom & top left* Bill Rothschild

Metric Conversion

Length

1 inch	25.4 mm
1 foot	0.3048 m
1 yard	0.9144 m
1 mile	1.61 km

Area

1 square inch	645 mm²
1 square foot	0.0929 m²
1 square yard	0.8361 m²
1 acre	4046.86 m²
1 square mile	2.59 km²

Volume

1 cubic inch	16.3870 cm³
1 cubic foot	0.03 m³
1 cubic yard	0.77 m³

Common Lumber Equivalents

Sizes: Metric cross sections are so close to their U.S. sizes, as noted below, that for most purposes they may be considered equivalents.

Dimensional lumber	1 x 2	19 x 38 mm
	1 x 4	19 x 89 mm
	2 x 2	38 x 38 mm
	2 x 4	38 x 89 mm
	2 x 6	38 x 140 mm
	2 x 8	38 x 184 mm
	2 x 10	38 x 235 mm
	2 x 12	38 x 286 mm
Sheet sizes	4 x 8 ft.	1200 x 2400 mm
	4 x 10 ft.	1200 x 3000 mm
Sheet thicknesses	¼ in.	6 mm
	⅜ in.	9 mm
	½ in.	12 mm
	¾ in.	19 mm
Stud/joist spacing	16 in. o.c.	400 mm o.c.
	24 in. o.c.	600 mm o.c.

Capacity

1 fluid ounce	29.57 mL
1 pint	473.18 mL
1 quart	1.14 L
1 gallon	3.79 L

Temperature

Celsius = Fahrenheit – 32 x ⅝
Fahrenheit = Celsius x 1.8 + 32

contents

safety first

Though all the designs and methods in this book have been reviewed for safety, it is not possible to overstate the importance of using the safest construction methods possible. What follows are reminders; some do's and don'ts of basic carpentry. They are not substitutes for your own common sense.

- *Always* use caution, care, and good judgment when following the procedures described in this book.

- *Always* be sure that the electrical setup is safe; be sure that no circuit is overloaded and that all power tools and electrical outlets are properly grounded. Do not use power tools in wet locations.

- *Always* read container labels on paints, solvents, and other products; provide ventilation, and observe all other warnings.

- *Always* read the manufacturer's instructions for using a tool, especially the warnings.

- *Always* use hold-downs and push sticks whenever possible when working on a table saw. Avoid working short pieces if you can.

- *Always* remove the key from any drill chuck (portable or press) before starting the drill.

- *Always* pay deliberate attention to how a tool works so that you can avoid being injured.

- *Always* know the limitations of your tools. Do not try to force them to do what they were not designed to do.

- *Always* make sure that any adjustment is locked before proceeding. For example, always check the rip fence on a table saw or the bevel adjustment on a portable saw before starting to work.

- *Always* clamp small pieces firmly to a bench or other work surface when using a power tool on them.

- *Always* wear the appropriate rubber or work gloves when handling chemicals, moving or stacking lumber, or doing heavy construction.

- *Always* wear a disposable face mask when you create dust by sawing or sanding. Use a special filtering respirator when working with toxic substances and solvents.

- *Always* wear eye protection, especially when using power tools or striking metal on metal or concrete; a chip can fly off, for example, when chiseling concrete.

- *Always* be aware that there is seldom enough time for your body's reflexes to save you from injury from a power tool in a dangerous situation; everything happens too fast. Be *alert!*

- *Always* keep your hands away from the business ends of blades, cutters, and bits.

- *Always* hold a circular saw firmly, usually with both hands so that you know where they are.

- *Always* use a drill with an auxiliary handle to control the torque when large-size bits are used.

- *Always* check your local building codes when planning new construction. The codes are intended to protect public safety and should be observed to the letter.

- *Never* work with power tools when you are tired or under the influence of alcohol or drugs.

- *Never* cut tiny pieces of wood or pipe using a power saw. Cut small pieces off larger pieces.

- *Never* change a saw blade or a drill or router bit unless the power cord is unplugged. Do not depend on the switch being off; you might accidentally hit it.

- *Never* work in insufficient lighting.

- *Never* work while wearing loose clothing, hanging hair, open cuffs, or jewelry.

- *Never* work with dull tools. Have them sharpened, or learn how to sharpen them yourself.

- *Never* use a power tool on a workpiece—large or small—that is not firmly supported.

- *Never* saw a workpiece that spans a large distance between horses without close support on each side of the cut; the piece can bend, closing on and jamming the blade, causing saw kickback.

- *Never* support a workpiece from underneath with your leg or other part of your body when sawing.

- *Never* carry sharp or pointed tools, such as utility knives, awls, or chisels, in your pocket. If you want to carry such tools, use a special-purpose tool belt with leather pockets and holders.

getting started

Design Considerations

Before you build a home for your car you must take note of your needs, your finances, and your building skills and determine what will be most appropriate. Do you want a garage or a carport? One that's joined to the house or one that stands alone? A one- or two-car size? Once you know what you'll build, you can go on from there.

Garage or Carport?

Choosing between a garage and a carport involves making decisions on architectural design, how much you want to spend, and what you want to use the structure for, other than providing your car with cover from the weather.

Garage. The advantages of a garage include the fact that it's an enclosed building that can be designed to complement your house's architecture and locked to provide reasonable security for the contents. In addition to its car-storing capacity, a garage may be equipped with closets or open shelf storage, workbenches, space for mowers, power tools, and the like. The garage may even have an area for a washing machine and dryer.

Carport. A carport is less expensive to build than a garage. The carport may be no more than a roof supported by wood, steel, or masonry columns. Alternatively, the structure may be enclosed on three sides and have an enclosed storage facility and workbenches.

Attached or Detached?

You may choose to build a garage or a carport that's independent of the house or attached to it. An independent, or detached, garage is a separate small building that's set a distance of a few feet to several yards from the house. A detached garage may be connected to the house with a covered breezeway. Some house designs, such as those with wraparound porches, look better with a detached garage.

An attached unit is joined to the house; most house designs permit attaching the carport or garage. The most convenient location is adjacent to the kitchen entrance, which makes carrying in groceries convenient. The attached unit provides direct access from car to house and vice versa without having to expose yourself to inclement weather. If your kitchen is located at the end of the house, the side of the lot must be wide enough to allow building within the setback distance required by your local zoning board. If the lot isn't wide enough, you may be able to use back yard space for the attached unit, provided a suitable entrance to the house is available.

Style and Materials

Whether you build an attached or detached carport or garage, keep the structure's design and materials compatible with the house. If the house has clapboard siding, apply that kind of siding to the unit. If the house has a contemporary flavor, design the garage in the same way. Make sure the garage or carport's roof pitch and window type match the house or complement it by echoing significant design elements.

Garage. Enclosed garages provide severe-weather protection and secure storage for your car and other possessions.

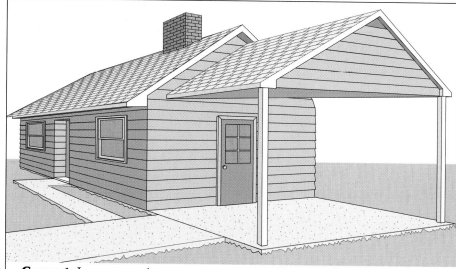

Carport. Less-expensive open carports provide cover for cars where security isn't a concern.

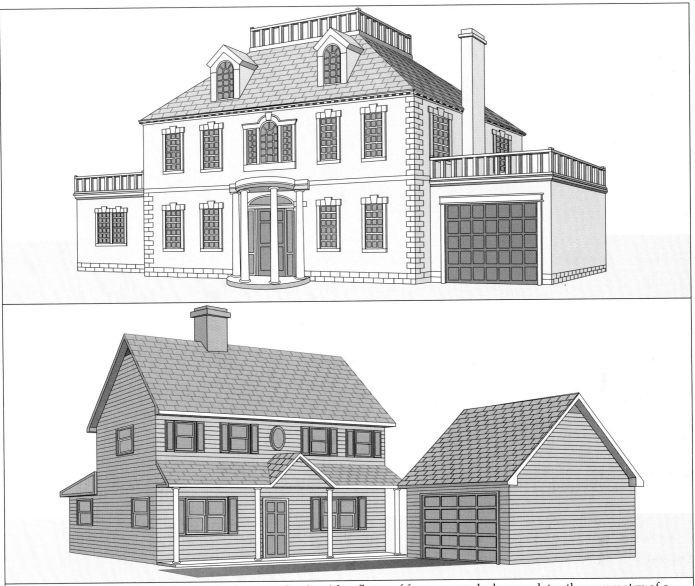

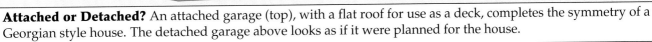

Attached or Detached? An attached garage (top), with a flat roof for use as a deck, completes the symmetry of a Georgian style house. The detached garage above looks as if it were planned for the house.

Style and Materials. When you build a garage, maintain the character of your current home. Use similar architecture, as well as siding and roofing materials. A garage attached by a breezeway seems to be part of the house.

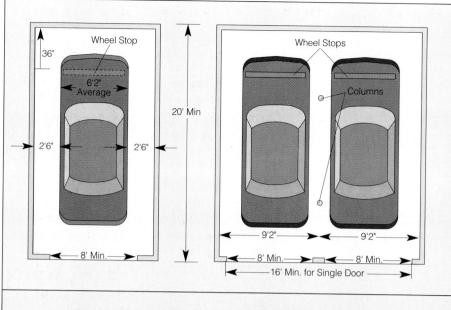

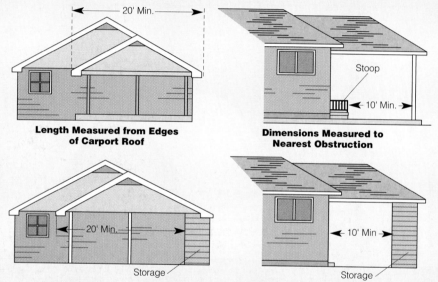

Length Measured from Edges of Carport Roof

Dimensions Measured to Nearest Obstruction

Storage

Storage

Standard Sizes. To make sure you'll have enough room for your car in your new garage or carport, follow the guidelines given here. Note that these are minimum dimensions. You can add to them, but don't build smaller.

Common Sizes for Garages and Carports

Structure Type	Length	Width
Minimum Dimensions		
One-car	20 ft.	10 ft.
Two-car	20 ft.	18 ft. 4 in.
Comfortable Dimensions		
One-car	23–24 ft.	12–15 ft.
Two-car	23–24 ft.	20–24 ft.

Garage Door Types & Sizes

Overhead garage doors have been greatly improved in the last few years and are available in wood, clad wood, steel, vinyl, and fiberglass. Steel and fiberglass doors may be insulated with rigid polystyrene or polyurethane foam cores, or they may be uninsulated. Vinyl doors have insulated cores to add rigidity. Most residential doors are sectional types and are available in raised panel, recessed panel, and flush styles with or without glass panes. Most insulated steel doors have an inner core of polystyrene or polyurethane. Many door styles are available in widths from 8 to 18 feet and in heights from 6 feet 6 inches to 8 feet. For convenience and an added measure of security, equip the garage door with the proper remote-controlled electric opener.

Building Department Requirements

Municipal and county building authorities generally prohibit erecting a garage or carport, attached or detached, without a building permit. You'll have to file an application with the local building department to get the permit.

An old carpenter, grumbling about the red tape involved in obtaining a building permit, suggested that the

Standard Sizes

When it comes to establishing the dimensions for your garage or carport (see "Common Sizes for Garages and Carports," above right), pay attention to the following guidelines:

■ Width and length are defined by the inside face of the studs of opposing walls and from the face of studs to the edge of the concrete entrance platform.

■ Where intermediate support posts are used in the width span of a two-

car garage or carport, provide a minimum spacing for automobiles of 9 feet 2 inches.

■ For easy entry and exit, allow a clearance space of 2 feet 6 inches between the sides of the car and any walls or other cars.

■ Locate any mechanical equipment where it's least likely to be damaged by vehicles. Laundry appliances won't fit in a minimum-size garage. Provide adequate clearance and working space for such equipment.

building department would soon require a floor plan and three sets of blueprints before a person could build a birdhouse. Although things are not quite that bad, you'll most likely have to submit some supplementary information, such as a site plan, floor plan, and elevations, along with the application.

Drawings

The first thing you'll need is a set of plans, or blueprints, and specifications for the project. The plans may or may not have to be prepared by an architect or engineer.

Plans are a graphic representation and are used as working drawings. Specifications provide detail information not provided on the plans. The plans, for example, might show a window opening as 2 feet 8 inches by 2 feet 10 inches. You would go to the specs to find that the window is a two-pane horizontal window with an aluminum frame and double-strength glazing.

The plans of your garage or carport project might be required to include:

■ A site plan

■ A floor and foundation plan

■ Elevations

■ Sections giving construction details

■ Any other information required by the building department

Draw plans clearly and to scale on quality paper. A scale of ¼ inch to 12 inches is a good one to use.

Site Plan

The site, or plot, plan usually comes under the jurisdiction of the zoning authority, which is separate from the building department. The plot plan describes the land on which you propose to build by legal description, street address, or similar description that precisely locates the site of construction. Include the section, block, and lot numbers if your locality uses them. A plan drawn to a scale of ¹⁄₁₆ inch to 1 foot is satisfactory.

The site plan should also contain the following:

■ Lot dimensions

■ Orientation to north

■ Dimensions for the front, side, and rear yards

■ Location and dimensions of the garage or carport

■ Location and dimensions of all easements, or legal right-of-way clearances

■ Location and dimensions of the house on the lot

■ Location and dimensions of all new construction, such as a driveway, a parking ramp, walks, a retaining wall, and the like.

Some jurisdictions may require you to show the grade elevation at the first floor of the dwelling and the floor of the new garage or carport. You may also have to show the elevation of the finished grade at each corner of the house

Additionally, the building department may require the elevation at the finish curb or crown of the street at the points of extension of the lot lines.

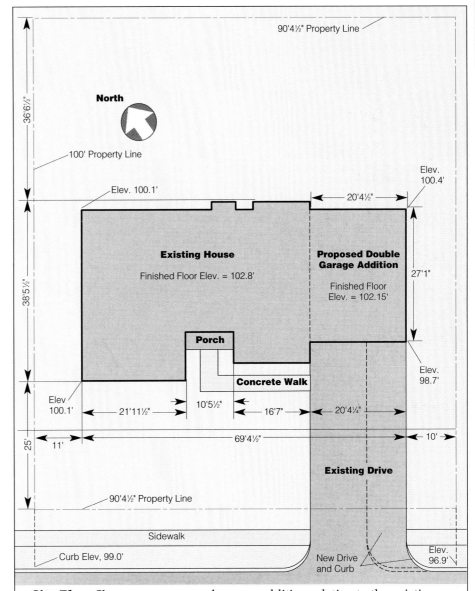

Site Plan. Show your proposed garage addition relative to the existing house and drive, if you have one, and show key elevations at the house corners and curb, as well as house and addition dimensions.

Depending on your lot, the department may even require elevations to show grading and drainage.

Setback. The requirements for setback from property lines vary from jurisdiction to jurisdiction. There are minimum setback distances for front, rear, and side yards, as well as a minimum distance between a dwelling and a detached garage or carport. Generally, detached units may be located within 5 feet of the rear property line, 10 feet of the side yard line, and 15 feet of the front property line. Consult your building department for specific setback requirements. The plot plan must show the setback dimensions.

Driveways. Most suburban homes have a driveway paved with concrete or asphalt. The driveway usually extends from the street pavement or curb line to the garage, carport, or parking space.

If you don't have a driveway, plan yours to have a minimum width of 11 feet with a flare at the entrance for incoming and outgoing turns. A curb opening of 14 feet is usually sufficient, but check with your local building authority. An opening of up to 18 feet wide may be required. If you're building a double garage or carport and pouring a double (two-car) driveway, be sure to show this on your plot plan. If it's a short driveway, you might wish to pour the drive the width of the two-car unit. Your building authority can advise you concerning the minimum width of a double-wide driveway, which may be 18 feet or less.

Variances. Most building departments allow variances in standards pertaining to the building site when an alternative method of plot planning is required to meet unusual circumstances, special topography, or design conditions on the site. If your plans fail to comply with all local building requirements, request a waiver. Department officials are often lenient toward carports and garages.

Floor Plan

In addition to the site plan, most building departments require at least a floor plan for carports and garages. Usually, the average homeowner can draw a sketch of the project to the satisfaction of the building inspector. Your department may, however, require that the plan view (and elevations) be prepared by a draftsman or architect.

The building department may require that your floor plan include:

■ Location and size of installed benches, cabinets, closet, shelves, plumbing fixtures, heaters, and the like

■ Direction, size, and spacing of all ceiling framing members, girders, columns, and piers

■ Location of all partitions, giving door sizes and direction of swing

■ Location, with proper symbols, of electrical equipment, including light fixtures, switches, and outlets

■ Location and types of permanent heating and cooling equipment, giving Btu capacity and electrical data

■ A foundation plan with a section drawing of the floor slab and footing

■ Sometimes, the layout of any heating/cooling ductwork, plumbing pipes, or other mechanical systems

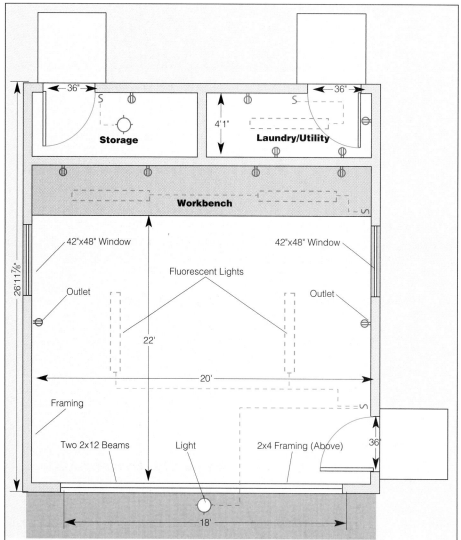

Floor Plan. Your building department may require that you show framing members, partition wall layout, electrical equipment with proper symbols, and location of heating and cooling equipment.

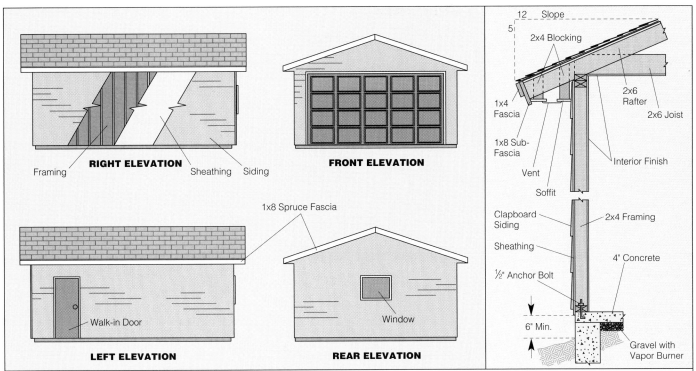

RIGHT ELEVATION
Framing   Sheathing   Siding

FRONT ELEVATION

1x8 Spruce Fascia

LEFT ELEVATION
Walk-in Door

REAR ELEVATION
Window

12 Slope
5
2x4 Blocking
2x6 Rafter
2x6 Joist
1x4 Fascia
Interior Finish
1x8 Sub-Fascia
Vent
Soffit
Clapboard Siding
2x4 Framing
Sheathing
4" Concrete
½" Anchor Bolt
6" Min.
Gravel with Vapor Burner

Elevations. Requirements for elevations are usually not as strict as for site plans and floor plans, so they can be simple. You may be required to show section details, however.

Elevations

The drawings you submit to the building department can be on a scale of ¼ inch to 12 inches for the main elevations and ⅛ inch to 12 inches for other elevations. The front, sides, and rear are considered main elevations. Other elevations include details and sections of specific parts of the structure.

Main elevation drawings typically show the following:

■ Location of windows and doors, giving the size

■ The type of exterior wall finish

■ The depth of wall footings, foundations, or piers

■ Finish floor lines

■ Finish grade lines adjacent to the building

In addition, if you're securing a construction loan through a government related mortgage, your building department may require the elevation drawings to include details and section drawings showing:

■ Section through exterior wall showing construction details at the footing and at the roof intersection in a minimum scale of ⅜ inch to 12 inches

■ Details of roof trusses, including connections and when they're required (in a scale of ⅜ inch to 12 inches, minimum), and stress or test data

Framing Plan

Your local building department or lending institution may also require a framing plan. The plan should show a pressure-treated sill plate on the floor slab or foundation wall, wall-stud spacing and height, ceiling joists, rafters, and a minimum one-by ridgeboard.

Fees and Inspections

A fee, established by the county or city, is charged for the building permit. Other fees may be assessed for such things as reinspection and additional plan review required by changes. A building permit will always require an inspection or

inspections of some sort. Your building department may call for as many as five inspections, depending on the jurisdiction.

Foundation Inspection. Once you've dug the trenches, erected the necessary forms, and had all materials for the foundation delivered on the job, you're ready for the inspector. The concrete you'll use to pour the footing does not have to be on the site.

Concrete Slab Inspection. This inspection is made after all in-slab or under-floor building service equipment, conduit, piping accessories, and other ancillary items are in place but before the floor slab is poured.

Frame Inspection. Schedule the inspector after the roof and all framing is in place, including fire blocking and bracing. All pipes and vent work must be completed and the rough electrical cable, plumbing pipes, and heating ducts installed.

Lath and Gypsum Board Inspection. If necessary, this inspection is made after all lathing and gypsum board is

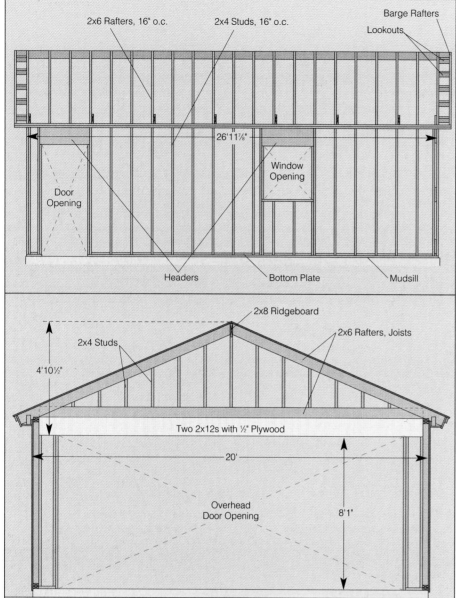

Framing Plan. If you have to submit a framing plan to your building department, show all framing members, including sills, plates, studs and spacing, headers, rafters, the ridgeboard, and overall dimensions.

To make an approved separation, use ⅝-inch X-type fire-resistant gypsum board on both sides of a 2x4 wood-frame wall separating the garage and the house. Apply the same board to the garage ceiling joists or the bottom chords of trusses. Masonry walls made of brick, block, tile, and the like also meet the requirement. Check with your local authority for guidelines.

An attached carport entirely open on two or more sides need not have a fire separation wall between the carport and the house. Windows between the carport and the dwelling should not be openable, however. Doors may be of any type, provided that any windows used in the door are fixed; doors between a dwelling and a carport should be self-closing.

Do the Work Yourself?

Before you decide to build a garage yourself, remember that any construction project involves a lot of physical labor—often hard labor. Also, certain abilities are prerequisite to complete a garage or carport successfully. You must know how to interpret plans, read a rule, use an assortment of power and hand tools, and the like. You'll learn some of these techniques in this book, but nothing takes the place of actual experience.

You should also consider the time involved. Building a carport or garage is more than a weekend project. Can you afford the time? A drawn-out construction project can become messy and disruptive to the family and neighbors.

If you're short on skill or time, you can hire a contractor to handle all the details and the construction. Or you can subcontract any portion of the work you cannot or prefer not to do, such as grading, excavating, and concrete finishing. When hiring a contractor, always get bids from at least three companies and check references.

in place but before any plastering is applied or before joints of the gypsum board and fasteners are taped and finished.

Final Inspection. The last inspection is made after finish grading and the building is completed and ready for use.

Further inspections are often required when the inspector finds a discrepancy that requires correction or when a portion of work for which inspection is called is not complete.

Fire Code for Attached Structures

According to most building codes, the garage or carport floor must be of approved noncombustible material, such as concrete. An attached garage must have a one-hour fire-resistant separation between it and the house. Doors into the house must have a solid core and be equipped with a self-closing device. Also, garages must never open directly into a sleeping room.

tools & materials

Tool Basics

This chapter should not be read as a wish list. For generations, carpenters—skilled craftsmen—managed quite well with little more than a hammer, a saw, some chisels, and a few planes. Except for the additions of the electric drill and circular saw, your toolbox doesn't need to include more than that same basic cache. Remember that power tools have been created for convenience—no one purchase will ever be able to replace skill, experience, and creativity.

Layout and Excavation Tools

Aside from the tools you'll use to mark and lay out the foundation, those you'd use for excavation are primarily limited to digging tools for postholes in a carport. For excavating a large garage, you may be better off hiring a contractor. One-time large jobs can also be done professionally and economically with rented tools.

Marking Out the Site

Measuring Tape. For garage and carport sitework, you'll find that a 25- or 30-foot tape will be the most useful for both long and short measurements.

Chalk Line. Nothing more than a roll of string held inside a chalk-filled container, a chalk line enables you to "snap a line" in only a couple of seconds. Stretch the string against a flat surface and pluck it to produce a straight, chalked layout line. Although red chalk may be a little easier to see, stick with blue. The red pigment is permanent and can stain anything with which it comes in contact (hands, wood, and such).

Plumb Bob. You can drop a perfectly vertical line from a given spot with a plumb bob. The heavy pointed bob is suspended on a string and is useful for aligning posts with pinpoint accuracy. Some chalk lines can also be used as plumb bobs.

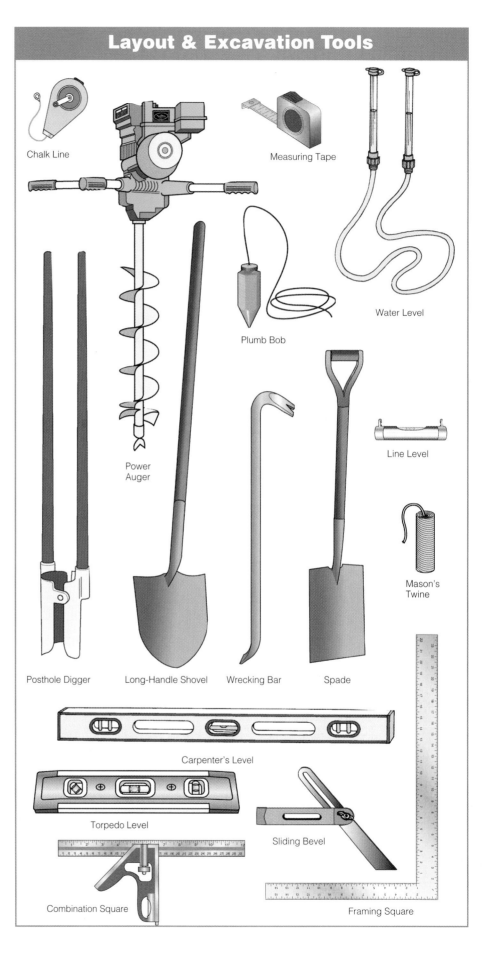

Layout & Excavation Tools

Chalk Line

Measuring Tape

Water Level

Plumb Bob

Line Level

Power Auger

Mason's Twine

Posthole Digger

Long-Handle Shovel

Wrecking Bar

Spade

Carpenter's Level

Torpedo Level

Sliding Bevel

Combination Square

Framing Square

Digging Tools

Posthole Digger. If you have to sink only a few posts or if you have a really strong back, you can dig holes by hand with a posthole digger. This double-handled tool is designed to cut deep, narrow holes and scoop out the dirt with clamshell-like blades.

Power Auger. For larger projects you'll thank yourself for renting a power auger to speed up the job. Power augers are powered by a gasoline engine and are essentially giant earth drills. Some models can be handled by one person; others require two. You'll still need a posthole digger to clean out the holes when you're finished with the auger.

Wrecking Bar. Also referred to as a breaking bar, you'll need this tool if you run into rock to break up the stone or to wedge it loose, whether you're using an auger or a posthole digger.

Long-Handled Shovel. This pointed shovel is good for digging and clearing out holes; the long handle enables you to dig deep.

Garden Spade. This flat-front shovel is useful for stripping sod from an area to be excavated. If you're going to excavate a large area—for a two-car garage's slab, for example—you'd be better off hiring an excavator or renting a backhoe.

Levels and Squares

Water Level. This level, intended for long spans, consists of a pair of clear graduated vials fitted onto a long tube—your garden hose will do. Water naturally seeks its own level; when the water levels in the two tubes are even, the points are level with each other. This is the most accurate method for measuring over long distances.

Line Level and Mason's Twine. Consisting of only a single vial, the line level is designed to be hooked to a string for leveling long spans. Make sure that the mason's twine, or string, is taut to ensure an accurate measurement.

Carpenter's Level. This level is a workhorse on any construction site. Available in 24- and 48-inch lengths, you'll use one for leveling and plumbing framing.

Torpedo Level. This small level is a good tool for plumbing up concrete forms and J-bolts as you set them in wet concrete. Its compact size makes it a handy addition to your toolbox.

Carpenter's Square. Also called a framing square, this large square is made from a single piece of steel or aluminum and is useful for laying out stair stringers and rafters.

Combination Square. The body of this adjustable square contains both 45- and 90-degree ends and can slide up and down the blade if you unlock the thumbscrew. The movable body makes this tool ideal for transferring depth measurements or running a line along a board.

Sliding Bevel. Probably the best tool for gauging and transferring angles other than 45 and 90 degrees is a sliding bevel, also known as a bevel gauge. A sliding bevel has a flat metal blade that can be locked into a wooden or plastic handle at any angle. A sliding bevel is great for transferring an existing angle on a project.

Cutting & Joining

Most people consider cutting and joining to be the most enjoyable part of carpentry. It's the hands-on work that they find satisfying—cutting and shaping wood to fit their design. That feeling of enjoyment will be enhanced if you work with the correct tools. More important, having the right tool for a specific job and knowing how to use it are the best ways to prevent injuries and avoid wasting material.

Circular Saw

This power tool has replaced the handsaw in almost every situation. That's because a circular saw is capable of crosscutting, ripping, and beveling boards or sheets of plywood quickly and cleanly. The most popular saws with carpenters and do-it-yourselfers alike are the models that take a 7¼-inch blade. This blade size will enable you to cut to a maximum depth of about 2½ inches at 90 degrees.

Choosing a Circular Saw. There are many options that distinguish one saw from another, the most important of which is its power. Don't judge a saw's performance by its horsepower rating, but by the amount of amperage that the motor draws. Low-cost saws may have only 9- or 10-amp

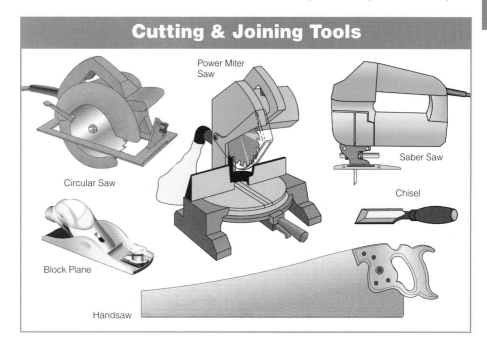

Cutting & Joining Tools

Power Miter Saw

Circular Saw

Saber Saw

Chisel

Block Plane

Handsaw

motors with drive shafts and arbors running on rollers or sleeve bearings. A contractor-grade saw is rated at 12 or 13 amps and is made with ball bearings.

Plastic housings are no longer the mark of an inferior tool; however, a thin, stamped metal foot is. Such a base won't stay as flat as a thicker base that's either extruded or cast. For safety's sake, be sure that your saw is double insulated to minimize any chance of electric shock.

Choosing a Circular-Saw Blade.
For general all-purpose use, carbide blades are the best for achieving smooth, precise cuts. Carbide blades may cost a few dollars more than a comparable blade made from high-speed steel, but you can expect it to remain sharp five times longer. A 24-tooth blade is usually adequate for general use.

Other Power Saws

Power Miter Saw. For angle cuts, you'll want to use this kind of saw, also called a chop saw or cutoff saw. These tools are simply circular saws mounted on a pivot assembly and are designed to make precise crosscuts.

Saber Saw. A saber saw can cut curves, make cutouts, and finish cuts started by a circular saw.

Hand Tools

Handsaw. For certain types of cuts, nothing will completely replace a good handsaw. A handsaw is just the thing whenever you have just a few cuts to do, for those spots where a circular saw can't reach, or when you want to finish off a circular-saw cut. A 15-inch saw with 10 to 12 teeth per inch (tpi) will cut well and still fit into your toolbox.

Block Plane. No matter how adept you become with your power tools, sooner or later you'll end up falling back on certain old reliables, like the block plane, to achieve close-fitting joints. A block plane is great to carry along with you on the site. A properly set plane will trim a shaving off at a

time from joint components, until the joint matches up perfectly.

Chisels. A set of three chisels, ¾ inch, 1 inch, and 1½ inches, will also be useful for close paring.

Other Required Construction Tools

There are a few tools that don't really fit into one specific category or that seem to apply to more than one category, and for that reason, they warrant their own special mention.

Electric Drill. For every project in this book, it's assumed that you have a drill—either electric or cordless. If you don't, you should pick up one with at least a ⅜-inch chuck, variable speed control, and a reverse switch. Make sure that your drill is sufficiently powered (3 amps, minimum) to handle the kind of abuse that it will receive on the job.

Cordless Drill-Driver. A cordless drill will provide you with all of the attributes of an ordinary drill, but without the hassle of having to drag around a long electrical cord. Use it to drill holes and drive screws.

Hammer. How can you build anything without a hammer? You can manage quite well with a standard 16-ounce finish hammer. When driving 12d or 16d nails into studs, beams, rafters, or joists, you'll quickly learn to appreciate the way a 20-ounce framing hammer can sink a nail in just a few blows.

Pry Bar. Available in a variety of sizes from 8 to 18 inches, pry bars have a notch at one end for removing stubborn nails. Pry bars are also useful as levers for coaxing hard-to-fit lumber, structural panels, and other building materials into place.

Cat's Paw. This variation on a pry bar is essential for removing deep-set nails mistakenly driven in framing lumber. It has a curved, slightly pointed head with a V-groove. When hit with a hammer, the head is driven below the surface of the wood to dig under nailheads.

Nail Set. With a nail set, you can countersink nails. Nail sets come in various sizes to match different types of nails; use the nail set sized to the nailhead being driven to avoid enlarging the hole.

Other Required Construction Tools

Tool Belt

Cordless Drill-Driver

Nail Set

Utility Knife

Pencils

Pry Bar

Folding Rule

Claw Hammer

Cat's Paw

Tool Belt. Unless you want to spend most of the day trying to remember where you left everything, a tool belt or work apron is a must. A good tool belt will have a spot for your hammer, measuring tape, chalk line, and block plane, and still have a pouch left over for nails and screws.

Utility Knife. This will probably be the most reached-for tool in your collection. You'll use the utility knife for everything from sharpening your pencil to marking cut lines to cutting shingles to shaving off wood to easing in a close-fitting joint.

Folding Rule. Anyone who's used a folding rule wouldn't be without it for measuring dimensions up to 72 inches. It's easy to use and extremely accurate over small distances.

Pencils. There's one thing that a carpenter can never have enough of—pencils, pencils, pencils.

Construction Fasteners

Throughout your garage or carport construction, you'll need a variety of nails, bolts, screws, and some framing hardware to join materials and strengthen joints. Metal fasteners will reinforce important joints like those between rafters and plates in structures subject to hurricane winds.

Nails

The most basic of metal fasteners is the nail. As commonly used, the term penny (abbreviated as d) indicates a nail's length. The number did not originally refer to the length of the nail but to the cost of 100 nails of that size. The length, diameter, head size, and approximate number per pound of the various penny sizes of common and finishing nails are listed in the table on the inside back cover of this book.

Common nails are preferred for general construction because they have an extra-thick shank and a broad head. Box nails are similar to common nails, but they have thinner shanks and don't have the holding power. Box nails are commonly used to attach sheathing, subflooring, underlayment, and other panel goods. You can purchase box nails that have been cement-coated (actually nylon-coated) to increase their holding strength. Their coating is melted by the friction of being driven through the wood, and it quickly resets. Try to drive cement-coated nails home in a few quick blows.

"Deformed" nails, such as helical, barbed, or ridged nails, also exhibit greater withdrawal resistance. These nails' shanks have been adapted to increase friction (helical nails are actually threaded like a screw) and have a 40 percent greater withdrawal resistance than common nails. Deformed nails are harder to drive.

If you don't want the nail's head to show, choose a finishing nail. Casing nails are similar to finishing nails but have a duller point and thicker shank; they have more holding power than a finishing nail of the same size. After the nail is driven nearly flush, both types can be sunk with a nail set. You can fill the hole with wood putty.

Sizing. When determining nail length, the general rule for softwoods is that the nail penetration into the bottom piece should be equal to or greater than the thickness of the top piece. For example, if you're nailing ¾- and ⅝-inch plywood to studs, use 8d box or common nails. For ½- and ⅜-inch panels use 6d nails. Space nails every 6 inches along the edges and 12 inches in the field. Ring- or screw-shank nails are recommended for this application to prevent the nails from working their way loose when the wood expands and contracts with moisture changes.

Screws

Bugle-Head Screws. Commonly known as drywall screws because they were originally developed for installing wallboard, these handy screws have become popular for all kinds of carpentry projects. Drywall screws have an aggressive thread and do not require a pilot hole. "Bugle Head" refers to the taper beneath the flat head of the screw that allows you to drive them flush in softwood and drywall without drilling a countersink hole. Screws have greater holding power than nails and can actually pull two boards tightly together. And because screws can be removed cleanly, they facilitate disassembly or the removal of a damaged board. But they cost considerably more than nails. As a result, screws are usually limited to two applications—installing plywood and drywall—though the possibilities are almost endless.

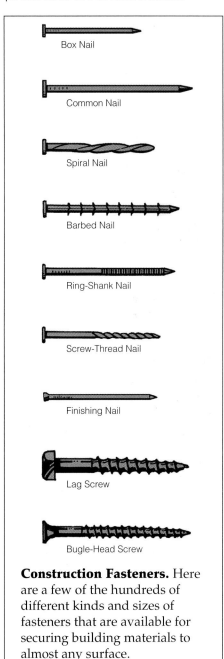

Box Nail

Common Nail

Spiral Nail

Barbed Nail

Ring-Shank Nail

Screw-Thread Nail

Finishing Nail

Lag Screw

Bugle-Head Screw

Construction Fasteners. Here are a few of the hundreds of different kinds and sizes of fasteners that are available for securing building materials to almost any surface.

Common sense should tell you not to do construction work without first having some basic safety equipment, such as eye and ear protection.

Always wear safety goggles or plastic glasses whenever you work with power tools or chemicals. Make sure your eye protection conforms to American National Standards Institute (ANSI) Z87.1 or Canadian Standards Association (CSA) requirements. Products that do will be marked with a stamp. Considering the cost of a visit to the emergency room, it doesn't hurt to purchase an extra pair for the times when a neighbor volunteers to lend a hand or when you misplace the first pair.

The U.S. Occupational Safety and Health Administration (OSHA) recommends that hearing protection be worn when the noise level exceeds 85 decibels (db) for an 8-hour workday. However, considering that a circular saw emits 110 db, even shorter exposure times can contribute to hearing impairment or loss. Both insert and muff-type protectors are available; whichever you choose, be sure that it has a noise reduction rating (NRR) of at least 20 db.

Your construction project will create a lot of sawdust. If you're sensitive to dust, it's a good idea to wear a dust mask. Two types of respiratory protection are available: disposable dust masks and cartridge-type respirators. A dust mask is good for keeping dust and fine particles from being inhaled during a single procedure. Respirators have a replaceable filter. Both are available for protection against nontoxic and toxic dusts and mists. Whichever you purchase, be sure that it's been stamped by the National Institute for Occupational Safety and Health/Mine Safety and Health Administration (NIOSH/MSHA) and is approved for your specific operation. When you can taste or smell the contaminate or when the mask starts to interfere with normal breathing, it's time for a replacement.

Work gloves are also advisable for avoiding injury to the hands. Catching a splinter off a board or developing a blister when digging postholes is not a good way to start a workday. Similarly, heavy-duty work boots will protect your feet. Steel toes will prevent injuries from dropped boards or tools. Flexible steel soles will protect you from puncture by a rogue nail.

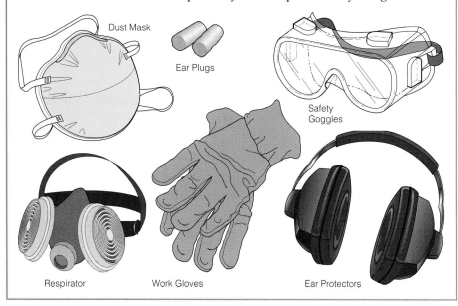

Dust Mask

Ear Plugs

Safety Goggles

Respirator

Work Gloves

Ear Protectors

In the United States, drywall screws are most readily available with Phillips heads. Some woodworking supply catalogs offer them with a square recess for driving the screws. Square-drive screws are more readily available in Canada. You'll need a power drill or driver to install drywall screws. The square drives are superior because you can't easily strip the drive hole or the bit. Drywall screws are available in a black oxide finish, suitable for interior work, and in a hot-dipped galvanized finish, for exterior construction. You'll usually find the exterior version sold as "deck screws." The most common lengths are 1, 1½, 2, 2½, and 3 inches.

Sizing. When determining screw length, the general rule for nail penetration applies. Though not recommended for framing, screws can be used effectively for installing sheathing. For ¾- to ⅝-inch plywood use a 1½-inch screw. For ½- to ⅜-inch plywood use a 1¼-inch screw. Space screws 12 inches along the edges and 24 inches in the field.

Lag Screws. Because they have a bolt-shaped head, lag screws are sometimes mistakenly called lag bolts, but unlike bolts, they don't protrude through the objects being joined. These heavy-duty fasteners are recommended for connections that must be extremely strong, such as where a ledger joins to the house in an attached carport. Lag screw lengths range from 2 to 12 inches, and diameters range from ¼ to ¾ inch in $\frac{1}{16}$-inch increments. Drill a pilot hole about two-thirds the length of the lag screw, using a bit ⅛ inch smaller than the lag screw's shank. Place a washer under each lag screw's head.

Metal Fasteners

You'll find many types of framing connectors in sizes to fit most standard-dimension rough and surfaced lumber. There are several major manufacturers of structural wood fasteners. Their basic product lines cover nearly all applications for standard framing. While an effort has been made to select the generic name for the fasteners described in this book, one manufacturer's hurricane clip may be another's storm tie. The fasteners you do buy may also look a little different from those illustrated. Just make sure they're designed to do the same job.

Nails for Fasteners. Most structural fastener manufacturers also supply nails sized and designed to provide maximum load performance when used with their fasteners. Since they are connecting sheet metal to wood, the nails can be shorter than if you were using a common nail to fasten together two boards of the same thickness. Use the number of fasteners and nails and the nailing pattern specified by the fastener manufacturer.

A. Post Anchors. These connectors secure the base of a load-bearing post to a concrete foundation, slab, or deck. In areas where there is a lot of standing water or rain, choose an elevated post base that raises a post 1 to 3 inches above the surface.

B. Joist Hangers. Joist hangers are used for butt joints between floor or ceiling joists and beams where they don't lap. Single- and double-size hangers are available. Rafter hangers are similar to joist hangers but are used to hang roof rafters from a ledger board, as in an attached carport with a shed roof.

C. Saddle Hangers or Purlin Clips. Available in single and double designs, these clips are ideal for installing crosspieces between joists or rafters.

D. Rafter Ties. These ties are used to provide wind and seismic ties for trusses and rafters.

E. Ridge Rafter Connector. These connectors resemble joist hangers with an open bottom. You can use them to fasten 2x6 rafters to ridge boards or ledgers. The open bottom can accommodate slopes up to 30 degrees.

F. Truss Plates. These plates are used in the construction of roof trusses. They can be designed with or without a lip. Various sizes are available.

Caution: *Not all plate-type fasteners are designed for truss applications. Be sure that the plates you buy are specified for roof truss construction. Special truss nails may also be required.*

G. Twist Tie. These straps are ideal for tying pieces that cross at 90-degree angles, such as joists, rafters, and beams.

H. Hurricane Ties. Use these ties to secure rafters and trusses to top plates. They use more nails than normal rafter ties for a stronger connection in hurricane-prone areas.

I. Panel Clips. These clips are slipped between the edges of plywood panels to lock them together where they span between rafters. Panel clips will also help maintain a sufficient gap between panels to allow for thermal expansion.

J. Post Caps. These fasteners can be used at the top of a post to join it to a beam or to strengthen a splice connection between two beams.

Metal Fasteners

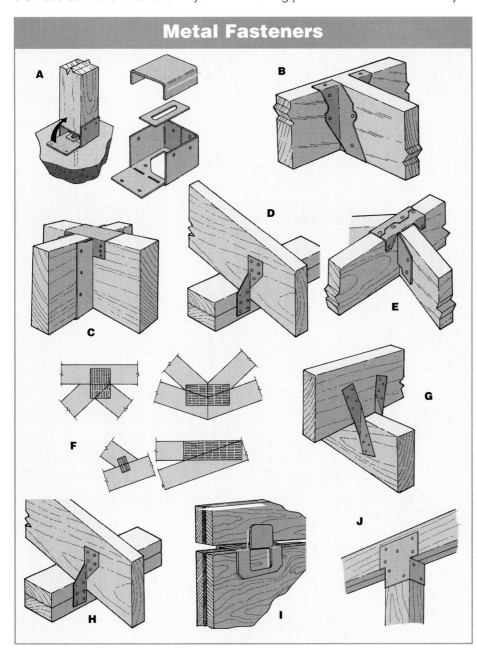

Lumber

Buying Lumber

Dimensioned softwood is sold by the lineal foot, in lengths of even 2-foot increments from 6 to 24 feet. Examine the ends of any critical-length lumber to make sure it's not slanted or damaged. You can't always count on the lumberyard to provide square ends, particularly on lower grades of lumber. If you have to square-cut the ends yourself, plan on losing ½ to 1 inch on both sides. For lumber that will be sized to smaller pieces, it's more economical to buy the smaller lengths than a single longer length.

Lumber Grades. The two major grades of softwood are select and common. Select lumber is also known as "clear" and has two good faces. Common grades, lower in quality than select, include 1, 2, 3, Const., Stand., Util., and Stud. You'll find that number 2 is most readily available and is suited for most general construction.

Lumber Defects

Bow. This defect is a deviation from a flat plane of the wide face, end to end. It has no effect on strength and can be used as long as you can nail it back to a flat plane.

Cup. A deviation from a flat plane of the narrow face, edge to edge, cupping tends to loosen fasteners.

Crook. A deviation from a flat plane of the narrow face, end to end, a crook generally makes wood unsuitable for framing. Minor crooks may be able to be pried straight and nailed in place.

Twist. This defect is a deviation from a flat plane of all faces, end to end, and makes lumber unsuitable for framing.

Check. Generally only cosmetic, a check is a rift in the surface caused by uneven drying.

Split. A serious structural weakness, a split is a crack that passes completely through the wood. Split lumber must not be used as a structural member.

Wane. The presence of bark or the lack of wood at an edge indicates a wane. Wane has little effect on strength, but any remaining bark should be removed, since the bark may promote rot.

Knot. The high density root of a limb, a knot is strong but can't be connected to any surrounding wood. The rules for knots in joists and rafters are 1) tight knots are allowed in the top one-third of the board width; 2) loose or missing knots are allowed in the middle; 3) no knots over 1 inch are allowed in the bottom one-third.

Decay. This is the destruction of the wood structure by fungi or insects, which prohibits any structural applications.

Pitch Pockets. Accumulations of natural resins in small areas, pitch pockets have little effect on lumber's structural strength.

Sizes of Lumber

Lumber	Nominal Size	Actual Size (inches)
Boards	1 x 3	¾ x 2½
	1 x 4	¾ x 3½
	1 x 6	¾ x 5½
	1 x 8	¾ x 7¼
	1 x 10	¾ x 9¼
	1 x 12	¾ x 11¼
Dimension Lumber	2 x 2	1½ x 1½
	2 x 4	1½ x 3½
	2 x 6	1½ x 5½
	2 x 8	1½ x 7¼
	2 x 10	1½ x 9¼
	2 x 12	1½ x 11¼
Posts	4 x 4	3½ x 3½
	4 x 6	3½ x 5½
	6 x 6	5½ x 5½

Lumber Defects

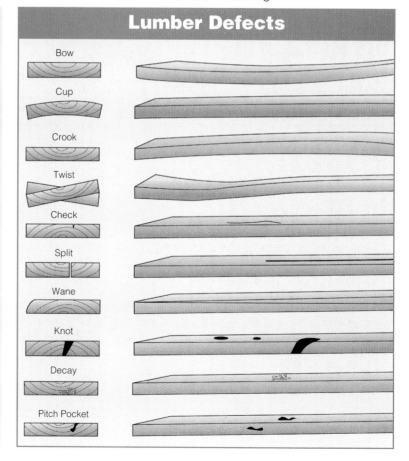

Bow, Cup, Crook, Twist, Check, Split, Wane, Knot, Decay, Pitch Pocket

chapter 3

siting & layout

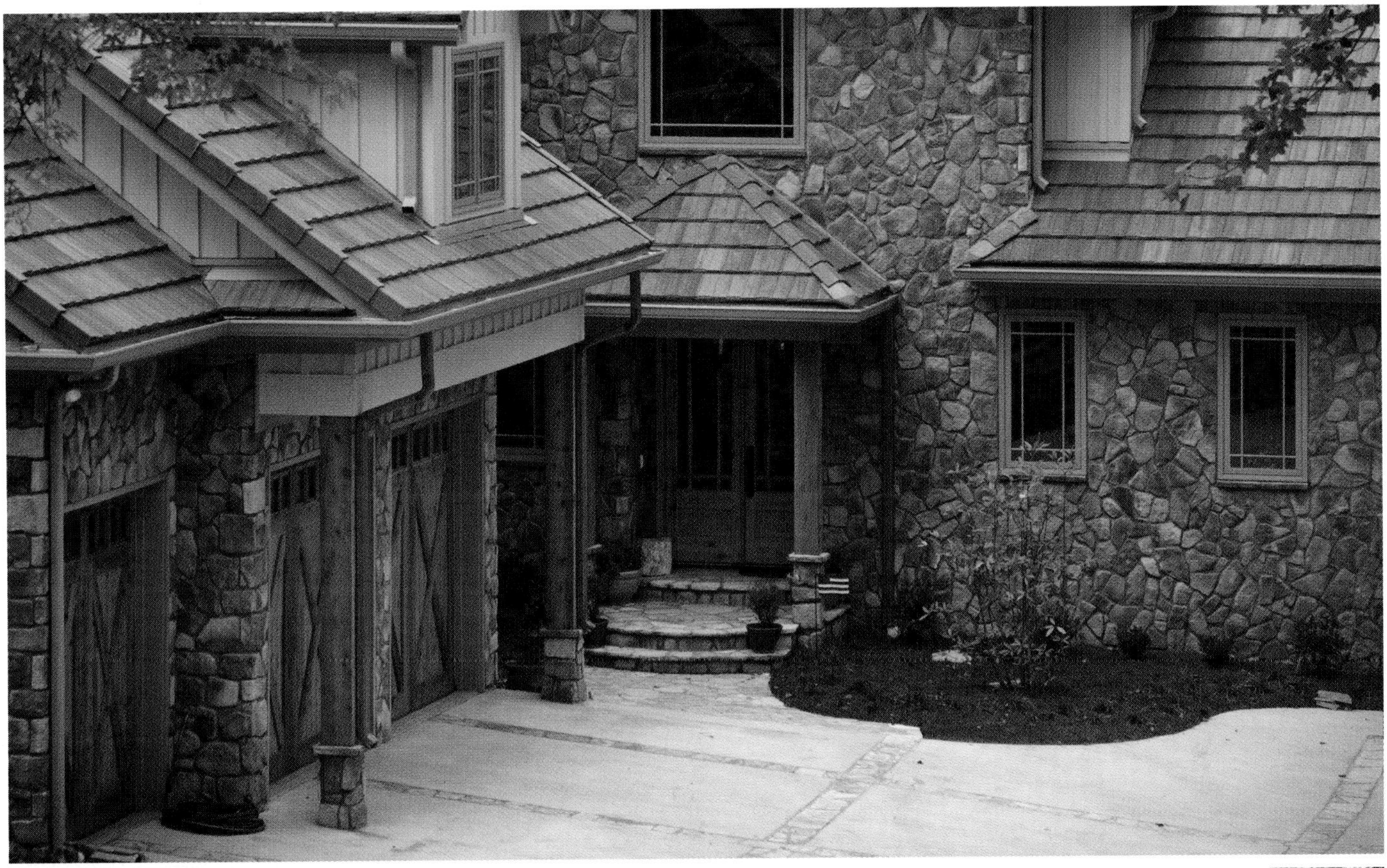

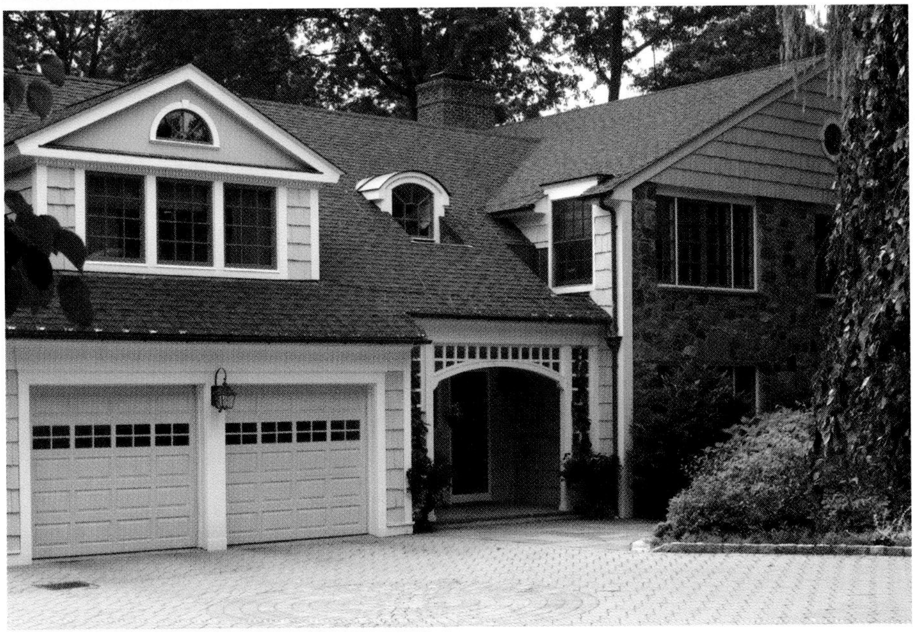

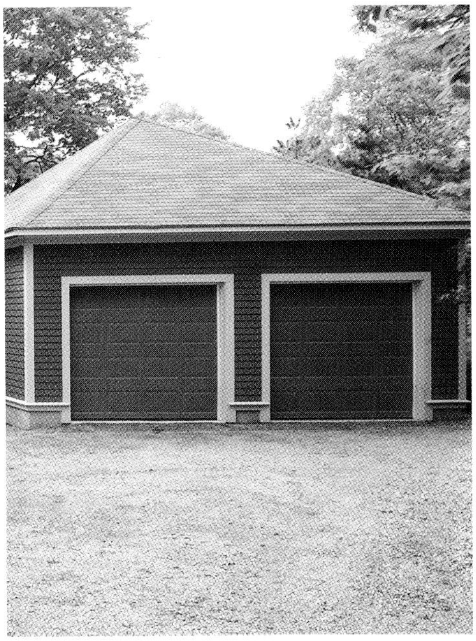

Structure Location

The style and floor plan of your home, the lot dimensions, unusual site conditions, and setback requirements will combine to dictate where and how you'll locate the garage or carport. The most difficult site is in the front yard. This is particularly true for an attached unit since it can seriously distract from the original house design.

Detached Units. A detached garage will normally be located to the side or rear of a house. For front yards, it's easier to site a detached garage or carport than an attached one—if there's enough space to build without blocking the view of the front of the house. A minimum distance of 10 feet is normally required between a dwelling and a detached unit. Most codes permit a minimum of a 5-foot distance when there are no windows located in the opposing walls.

Attached Units. The most practical location for attached units is immediately adjacent to the kitchen entrance.

For many home styles, this location is at the end or in the rear of the house. A double garage can include laundry and storage space with convenient access to the kitchen. The house floor plan and style may also permit offsetting the garage.

If space permits, orient the garage so that the entrance doesn't face the street. This way, the view from the front will not be dominated by a large garage door. In addition to the aesthetic advantage of having the door out of immediate view, you'll maintain

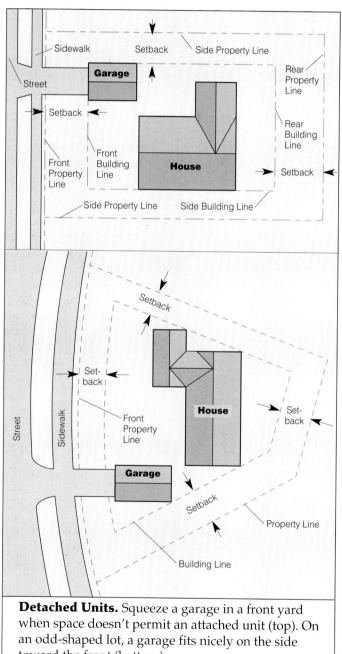

Detached Units. Squeeze a garage in a front yard when space doesn't permit an attached unit (top). On an odd-shaped lot, a garage fits nicely on the side toward the front (bottom).

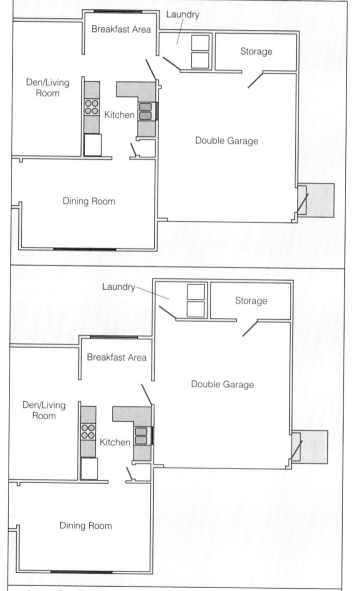

Attached Units. The most practical location for an attached garage is immediately off the kitchen (top). You can also offset the garage to make it even more convenient (bottom).

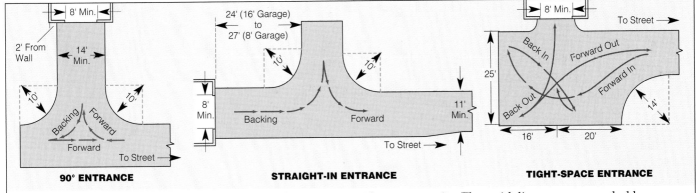

Turnarounds. Provide a turnaround in front of the garage if space permits. The guidelines recommended by architects are shown for three entrance configurations.

your privacy should you choose to leave the garage door open.

Parking. A well-planned garage location provides for sufficient space in front of the building to park a vehicle in the driveway a) without blocking the sidewalk and b) leaving sufficient space in front of the car to allow a walkway and to operate the garage door. Avoid steep slopes immediately in front of the structure if possible. The first 20 to 25 feet of the driveway should slope no more than 2 percent, or about ¼ inch per foot.

Turnarounds. If space permits, provide a turnaround area for additional parking and to avoid having to back out into the street when leaving. Turnarounds can be designed both for garages that face the street and for those that are offset from the street.

Making a Site Plan

1 **Marking the Property Lines.** Use grid paper to make your plan. A scale of ¼ inch to 48 inches should suffice. Start by marking the property lines. Indicate north, south, east, and west. Check with the local building department to find out how far the structure must be set back from the lot lines. Mark these setback limits as dotted lines on your plan.

2 **Locating Existing Structures.** Starting from a front corner of the house, measure the dimensions of the house, and transfer them to the plan. Include the locations of exterior doors and windows on the wall or walls facing the garage or carport. Measure and mark the locations of other buildings and permanent structures, including patios, decks, fences, and concrete walks. Show any under-ground or overhead fixtures, such as utility lines and septic systems.

3 **Locating Plantings.** Mark the locations of trees, shrubs, and other major plantings, and specify which ones you'll keep and which you'll remove or relocate. On sloping sites, the building department may require you to indicate spot elevations or grade contours. The finished site plan will serve as your base map

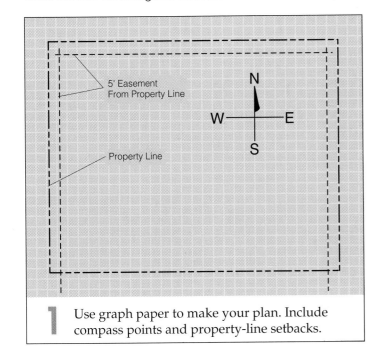

1 Use graph paper to make your plan. Include compass points and property-line setbacks.

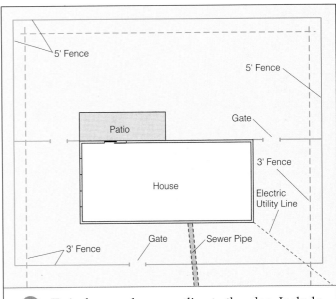

2 Transfer your house outline to the plan. Include any other structures and underground fixtures.

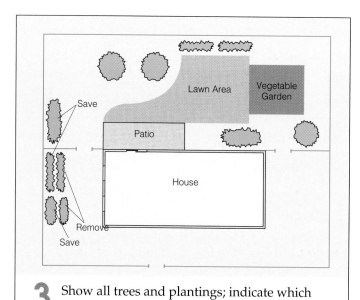

3 Show all trees and plantings; indicate which ones will be in the way and must be removed.

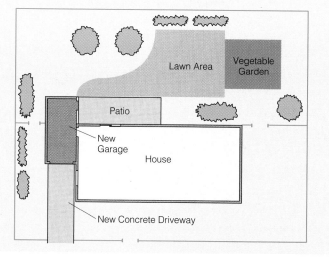

4 Use an overlay to draw in the garage or carport location and show how it relates to the property.

for locating the garage or carport and driveway.

4 **Locating the New Structure.** Attach an overlay of tracing paper to the base map. Draw in the exact size and location of the proposed garage or carport, including the driveway, doors and windows, new utility lines, new plantings, and any walks leading to the garage. Use as many overlay sheets as needed to come up with a suitable plan. Draw the final overlay neatly, and submit it with your base map when you apply for a building permit.

Foundation Layout

Using Batter Boards

One of the most important aspects of building a garage or carport is starting with square corners. If you don't, nothing will fit as it should, including the rafters (or trusses), sheathing, and roofing. Using batter boards made with 1x4 or 2x4 material provides a means not only of ensuring a square foundation layout but also of gauging the depth of the footing excavation and footing thickness.

For a detached garage, batter boards are required for each corner. For an attached unit, you'll need batter boards for each corner not connected to the house. For corners of the garage joining the house wall, a nail driven into the wall at this point will suffice to hold the layout strings.

An attached garage is squared with the house wall and thereby has fixed corners. The two or three "free" corners are those that can be adjusted to square up the unit. In detached units, the front of the structure is commonly lined up with the street or house. The front corners are, therefore, fixed in position. Any adjustments required for squaring will be limited to the two rear corners.

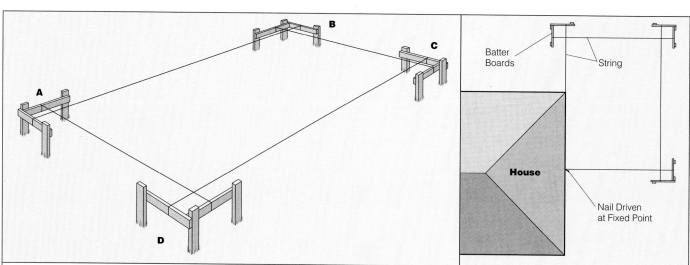

Using Batter Boards. Locate four corners of a detached garage or carport using batter boards. When joining one to the house, use batter boards to locate the corners not attached to the existing building.

1. Setting Up Batter Boards.

Choose one corner of the garage near the house, and mark it by driving a stake into the ground. The stake should mark the outside of the building lines. Use 1x4s or 2x4s as stakes for the batter boards. Locate three stakes as shown in the drawing 48 to 72 inches back from the building line to allow space for trenching and foundation work. Use a framing square to locate the batter-board stakes reasonably close to a 90-degree angle. Attach 1x4s horizontally to the stakes. Erect the batter boards at approximately a 24-inch height.

2. Placing the Second Stake.

Cut a saw kerf into the board that's at right angles to the structure to which you're orienting the garage; tie a knot in the end of a nylon string, and wedge the string into the kerf; then stretch the string parallel with the structure across the first stake. Measure the desired dimension of the garage or carport along the string, and drive another stake. Set up batter boards the same way as in Step 1.

3. Measuring with the 3-4-5 Triangle.

Measure along the line 3 feet from the first stake (A), and mark the string at this point (B). From stake A, run a second line perpendicular to the first. Measure out 4 feet to locate point C. If this second line is exactly at a right angle to the first, the diagonal between the 4-foot point C and the 3-foot point B will be exactly 5 feet. If it's not 5 feet, move point C left or right until the diagonal measures 5 feet, and stake that point. Any multiples of the 3-4-5 triangle, such as 6-8-10 and 9-12-15, provide the same results. Now stretch the string from stake A across stake C, and fasten the string to a temporary stake located outside the intended garage or carport area.

4. Outlining the Garage.

Measure along the string from point A, and mark the garage dimension in that direction using a stake and batter boards. Use the 3-4-5 triangulation method to extend another line at a

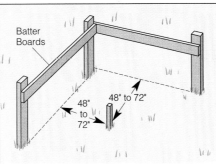

1 A stake marks the corner of the structure. Set three stakes 48 to 72 in. from the corner stake, and attach 1x4 batter boards.

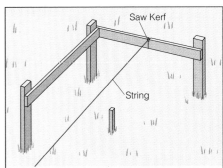

2 Cut a saw kerf in the batter board, and insert a string. Measure off the building's dimension, and set a second stake.

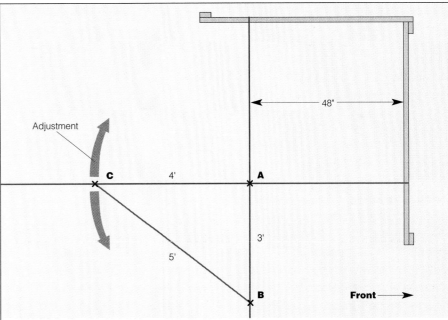

3 Starting at A, measure 3 ft., and mark point B. Measure 4 ft. at a right angle to AB, and locate C. Move C until it's exactly 5 ft. from B.

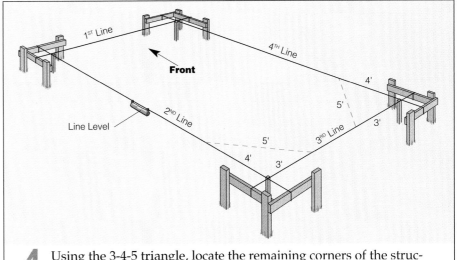

4 Using the 3-4-5 triangle, locate the remaining corners of the structure to finish the building outline.

right angle to the line you just set, parallel with the first line. Measure to the next corner and stake it, and finish by setting up the last line with the 3-4-5 triangle. Double-check the accuracy of the layout by measuring the diagonals between opposite corners. If the measurements are equal, all corners are at right angles. Once you've attached all of the strings and you've made sure that they're square, adjust the height of the batter boards so that all strings are level. You can accomplish this task by hanging a line level from each string.

Laying Out Walls

To lay out the wall line, drop a plumb bob at each string corner. Drive a small stake at that point. This is the outside corner of the garage and can represent the outside surface of the studs or the finish wall line for masonry veneer.

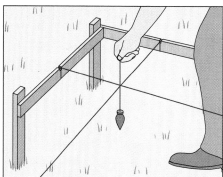

Laying Out Walls. Adjust the strings to represent the finish wall line. Drop a plumb bob to locate the exact outside corners.

Laying Out Footings

A garage footing may be flush with the outside of the stud wall or extend beyond the stud wall to accommodate a brick or stone finish. If you want the footing flush with the wall line, pull a string from the stakes marking the wall line, and measure the footing width inward from the string. Drive stakes and pull a string to establish the inside line of the footing.

When laying out a footing extending beyond the wall line, establish the outside edge by measuring from the wall line stakes at each corner. Drive small stakes at this position, and pull a string between the stakes. Establish the footing width by measuring inward from the string.

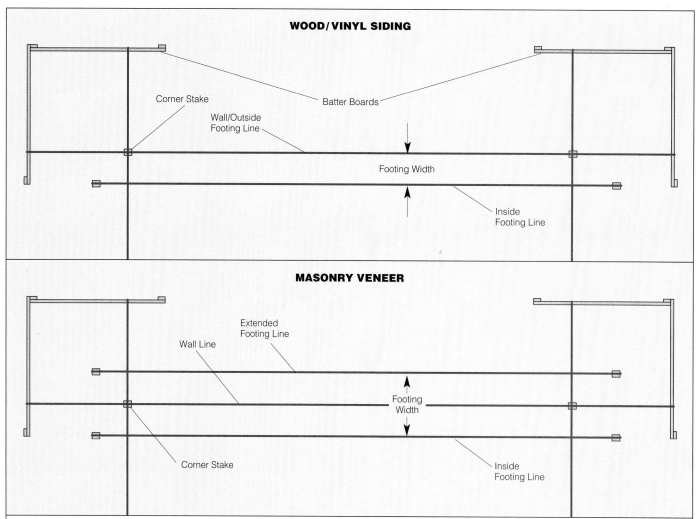

WOOD/VINYL SIDING

Corner Stake

Batter Boards

Wall/Outside Footing Line

Footing Width

Inside Footing Line

MASONRY VENEER

Extended Footing Line

Wall Line

Footing Width

Corner Stake

Inside Footing Line

Laying Out Footings. To lay out the footings, you must know what material the siding will be. For conventional wood or vinyl siding, the footing is flush with the exterior wall line (top). For brick or masonry veneer, extend the footing beyond the wall line (bottom).

foundations

Site Excavation

Clear the construction area, removing all shrubs, rocks, and other obstacles that aren't part of your design. The extent of the excavating work depends on the site. The job usually calls for mechanical power equipment. In fact, leveling and excavating for a two-car garage or carport can take on major proportions and is often best contracted to someone with the proper equipment and expertise. Minor excavation for a shallow slab and footing may be dug by hand if you're in shape and don't mind the "exercise." In general, you'll trench for the footing before excavating for the floor slab.

Footings

You must install footings below the frost line. Consult your building department to determine the required depth. Depending on your location, the frost line may be as deep as 48 inches. However, even in areas with no frost line to speak of the excavation should extend at least 6 inches below the finish grade for optimal stability.

The depth of the frost line in your area may require that a foundation wall be constructed to bridge the dimension between the footing and the floor slab.

In firm soil, you may dig the footings with vertical sides the exact width of the footing to eliminate the need for forms. Footings may be dug by hand or with a backhoe that has the correct-size bucket. Support columns, which you might use in a carport or in a two-story two-car garage to support a floor overhead, require pier footings. (See page 32.)

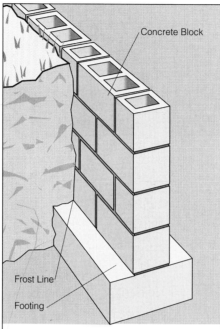

Footings. You must install a footing below the frost line for your area. A concrete-block or poured-concrete foundation stem wall may sit on top of the footing.

If it's required, the foundation-wall trench must be wide enough to provide space for erecting concrete forms or laying block. Allow about 24 inches beyond the wall line for this.

Setting the Floor Level

To ensure wood framing members and siding remain free of ground contact and moisture, and to prevent flooding of the floor, the top of the garage and carport floor must be a minimum of 6 inches above the finish grade.

Don't over-dig the footing or floor area. Firm, undisturbed soil is required underneath. Any backfill must be firmly tamped to prevent voids under the concrete. When excavating or leveling the floor area, keep in mind that the floor slab, usually 4 inches thick, is poured over a 4-inch-thick base bed of gravel, crushed stone, or sand.

Providing Drainage

Low-lying areas often have drainage problems. Soils with a poor percolation, or seepage, rate can also cause problems. Before you build, consult with an engineer or soils scientist to determine the ability of the ground to absorb or carry off surplus water. Your local building department can give you information on soils scientists in your area.

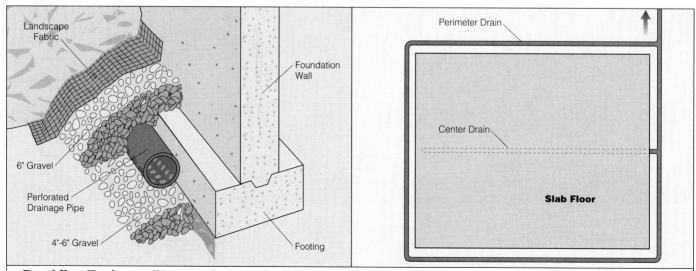

Providing Drainage. Divert underground water with 4-in. perforated drainpipe. Install the drainpipe in a bed of gravel under the slab and around the perimeter to carry water to a natural fall or sewer.

If you have poorly draining soil, the problem can be more underground than above ground due to hydrostatic pressure that forces ground water up against the floor and footing from below. To avoid the problem, install a 4-inch perforated plastic drainpipe at the footing level in a bed of gravel. Orient the perforations in the drainpipe downward. Pour a minimum of 4 to 6 inches of gravel under the pipe and at least 6 inches over it. Cover the gravel with a layer of hay or landscaping fabric to prevent soil from clogging up the gravel. Lay the drainpipe the full perimeter of the structure, and run it to a sewer drain or natural fall-off point.

Hydrostatic pressure can be tremendous under a concrete slab. To relieve the pressure and prevent water damage to the floor (or seepage into the garage), install a 4-inch perforated drainpipe in a full bed of gravel along the length of the floor.

Constructing a garage or carport, attached or detached, is not going to affect the ground-level drainage capability of your lot to any appreciable degree. The contour is set, and if there's currently no drainage problem, you'll have nothing to be concerned about if you slope the finish grade away from the unit and the house.

Placing Concrete

Concrete is made by mixing water with portland cement, sand, and coarse aggregate such as gravel. Considering the amount of concrete you'll require for your footings, floor slab, and in some cases driveway, you should probably order ready-mix concrete from a concrete supplier. If you're using separate footings, you'll have to pour the footings a week or more before the slab and driveway to allow them to cure properly, so you may have to arrange for two or more deliveries.

Take a little time to consider exactly what this step of the job entails. Concrete should be placed within 20 minutes after mixing is completed. The

initial set occurs in about 20 minutes in warm weather, and you shouldn't disturb the concrete after the initial set. To do so will cause the concrete to lose considerable strength. The transit time of ready-mix is considered mixing time, and the "set" time doesn't begin until after the concrete is placed.

Plan to work in good weather. Late spring or early fall are good times for concrete work because there's usually no threat of freezing or drying out the concrete. Also, you and your workers won't have to contend with the hot summer sun.

Assembling a Crew. You won't be able to handle a large volume of truck-delivered ready-mix concrete working alone. Assemble a crew of at least two helpers. Always have at least one helper with some experience in floating, final troweling, and edging. An experienced concrete finisher will keep the project moving and serve as an adviser to less experienced crew members. Another idea is for you to do all the preparation—layout, form building, and subgrade preparation—then hire a professional to handle the concrete placement.

Planning for Delivery. If you plan to do the work yourself, discuss the project with someone at the ready-mix plant. He or she should know the local codes and the concrete specifications used in your area. Also be sure to check with the building inspector. You'll probably need a permit, and the inspector can let you know in advance if your plans follow code.

Plan ahead for choice delivery times, such as Saturday mornings, and know the procedure for canceling delivery if the weather fails to cooperate. A delivery truck can tear up a lawn or sink into fresh fill, so be sure the truck will have access to your site without causing these kinds of problems.

Ordering Ready-mix. Ready-mix concrete is delivered to the site ready to pour. Concrete is measured by the

cubic yard. To estimate the quantity of concrete required for a footing, use this formula: Multiply the length of the footing in feet times the width in feet times the thickness in inches; then divide by 314. The result will be a slightly generous estimate of the cubic yards of concrete you'll need, ensuring that you won't run short.

Assume your garage is 22 x 24 feet and that it will have an 18-inch wide footing 6 inches thick:

$$
\begin{array}{r}
92 \text{ feet (length)} \\
\times \quad 1.5 \text{ feet (width)} \\
\hline
138 \text{ square feet} \\
\times \quad 6 \text{ inches (thickness)} \\
\hline
828 \text{ divided by } 314 \\
\text{equals } 2.6 \text{ cubic yards.}
\end{array}
$$

Note that the corners are counted twice, allowing for waste and the invariable low spots found in most trench work. Most plants figure in quantities of ¼ cubic yard, so round up the sum to 2 ¾ cubic yards.

You can also use the formula to estimate quantities for slabs. For the above garage, 24 feet (length) times 22 feet (width) equals 528 square feet. Multiply 528 by 4 inches (thickness), which equals 2,112. Divide 2,112 by 314, and the result is 6.73. You'd order 6 ¾ cubic yards of ready-mix concrete.

Pouring and Curing Considerations. Pour ready-mix from the truck or wheelbarrow as close to the final place as possible to avoid segregation of aggregates and honeycombing often caused by raking or pushing the concrete a distance from where it's initially poured. Also, avoid overworking concrete in forms. Such "petting" causes the finer materials and the cement base to work toward the top, with the larger aggregates dropping to the bottom.

After about 7 days the concrete will have gained most of its strength and will be safe to drive on. It helps to keep the concrete surface wet during this time by sprinkling it with water or covering it with wet burlap. A chemical compound may be added at the plant that slows down the drying process so you don't have to be so meticulous about keeping the concrete wet.

Forming Perimeter Footings

For many footings in firm soil, no forms are necessary. The trench sides are stable enough to serve as a natural form. Cut the footing trench with smooth, vertical sides, and pour concrete directly into the trench. In sandy and unstable soils, you'll have to build forms as described in the steps below. Where footings extend above the grade level and form foundation walls as well, forms are required for that part of the concrete above grade.

Keep footing forms as simple as possible. Footings range in width from 8 to 18 inches. Check with your building department on local requirements.

1 **Digging the Trench.** Excavate the footing trench to the proper width and depth using your batter boards and strings as guides. To keep the trench depth consistent, drop a plumb bob at frequent levels along the batter-board strings around the garage's perimeter. Remember that the original string locations represent the outside walls of the garage; you must position the trench and the foundation forms so that the outside edges of the mudsills will align with the strings.

2 **Building the Forms.** Construct the forms as shown. Note that there are two configurations; choose the one that matches your situation. For shallow footings, the footing thickness should equal the width of the boards plus ½ inch. A 12-inch-thick footing, for example, uses 2x12s suspended ½ inch above the bottom of the trench. It's okay if some concrete spills out beneath the forms, becomes this will help provide a more solid base for the footings. Nail the boards to 1x2 or 2x4 stakes spaced 18 to 24 inches apart. Attach 1x2 braces across the top of the forms every 24 inches to keep them from spreading when you pour the concrete. If you're building the form as a monolithic footing/foundation wall, its top must be at least 6 inches above ground level. Make sure the inside and outside corners of the forms meet at right angles. Before you pour the concrete, brush the insides of the forms with a light coating of motor oil to make them easier to remove after the concrete cures.

3 **Pouring the Concrete.** Suspend steel reinforcing bars (rebars) a couple of inches above the bottom of shallow trenches to increase the footing's resistance to bending and pulling forces caused by temperature extremes such as ground freezing. Rebars are available in ¼-, ⅜-, ½-, ⅝-inch and larger diameters

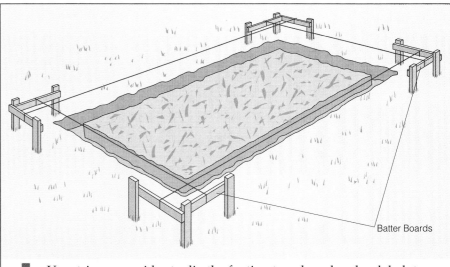

Batter Boards

1 Use strings as guides to dig the footing trench and a plumb bob to help maintain a consistent depth.

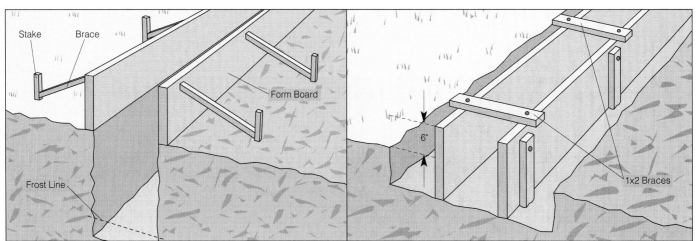

Stake   Brace

Form Board

Frost Line

6"

1x2 Braces

2 For deep footings dig a trench and use formwork only for that part of the concrete that extends above the ground. For shallow footings, make concrete forms from two-by boards secured with 1x2 or 2x4 stakes.

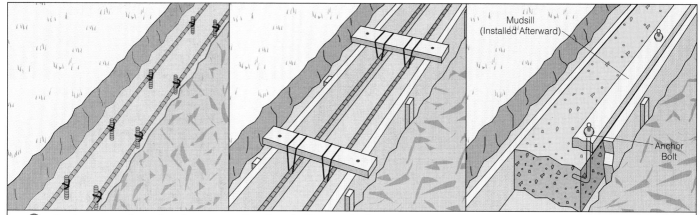

3 In deep trenches, tie rebar to steel stakes (left). For shallow footings, hang the rebar from cross braces using tie wire (middle). For footing/foundation walls, set anchor bolts every 24 inches once you've poured the concrete but before it dries (right).

and in lengths up to 20 feet. Consult your building department for the size required. Wire the rebar to steel rebar stakes in the trench or hang it from the formwork cross braces, as shown in the drawings. Another method, which requires less labor and cost, involves pouring about 2 inches of concrete into the footing, placing the bars in position on top of this layer, then completing the pouring. Regardless of the method used, position the bars to overlap at the corners. Pour wet concrete flush to the top of the forms, using a shovel or hoe to work out any air pockets. Use a wood float, flat trowel, or short length of 2x4 to screed and smooth the top of the footing. If you're pouring a footing/foundation wall, insert anchor bolts every 24 inches, as shown.

Pouring Post Footings for Carports

Attached carports are often supported on one side by columns or posts instead of a wall. Detached units may be supported entirely by columns. The posts may be centered on piers having independent footings. A concrete pier footing 12 inches square and 6 inches thick placed below the frost line is generally sufficient in firm soil. A pier footing 16 inches square and at least 6 inches thick may be required by codes in weaker type soils.

If you need to make only a few footings for piers, you can mix your own concrete from sacks of dry mix. One 90-pound sack will make 2/3 cubic

foot of concrete, enough for one 12 x 12 x 8-inch footing.

1 **Locating the Corner Footing Holes.** Using the string and batter boards and a plumb bob as a guide, locate a footing hole at each corner that requires a post. Drive a stake into the ground to mark the spot. Remember that the intersections of the strings represent the outside corners of the carport floor; dig the footing holes so that the outside corners of the posts, when attached to the footings, will align with the intersecting strings.

2 **Locating Intermediate Footing Holes.** Measure along each string to locate the rest of the footing holes between the corner holes. Drop

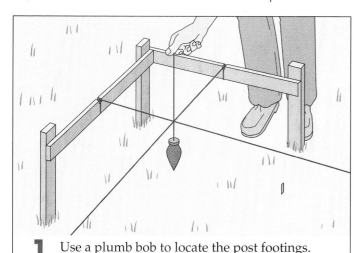

1 Use a plumb bob to locate the post footings. The plumb bob's point represents the outside corner of the post once it's set in the footing.

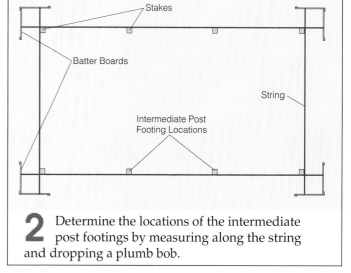

2 Determine the locations of the intermediate post footings by measuring along the string and dropping a plumb bob.

a plumb line at each location, and mark the spot with a stake.

3 Digging Footing Holes. Use a long-handled shovel, post-hole digger, or rented power auger to dig holes at the staked positions. For adequate support, the footing hole must extend at least 6 inches below the surface of the ground or below the frost line. If you're digging the holes in loose soil, compact the bottom using a hand tamper.

4 Installing Pier Blocks. If you're using precast pier blocks, pour wet concrete into the holes within 3 to 6 inches of ground level. While the concrete is still plastic, but stiff enough to support the weight of a pier without its sinking, embed the pier 1 to 2 inches into the footing, aligning the

outside edges of the blocks to the batter-board strings. The top of the pier block should be at least 3 inches above ground level. Place a level diagonally across the top of the pier in both directions to level it.

You can also use a ready-made cardboard pier form. The form consists of a waxed cardboard tube that keeps the surrounding soil from falling into the space where the concrete will be poured. Tubes are available in a variety of sizes. Make the diameter of the posthole a bit bigger than that of the tube. Cut off the tube a little above the level you want the concrete to be, using a handsaw or saber saw. Place the tube in the hole, and compact soil around it to make it stable. Brace the tube if necessary; then fill it with concrete up to a few inches above grade.

5 Leveling the Pier Blocks. Before the concrete has a chance to cure, level the piers to the same height with a line level and string. Adjust the pier heights by adding more wet concrete, if necessary, to raise them.

If you're using forms, smooth the concrete, and insert a post anchor or other metal connector at the right height. Use a level to make sure the connector is vertical. When you install the posts, avoid water damage and rot by raising the posts off the bottom of the anchors by less than ¼ inch. Cut a double-thick scrap of asphalt shingle to serve as a spacer under the post.

Foundations

The foundation rests directly on the footing. The purpose of the foundation

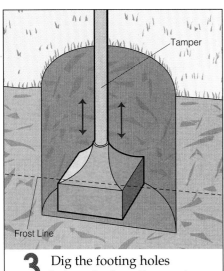

3 Dig the footing holes below the frost line, and tamp the bottom.

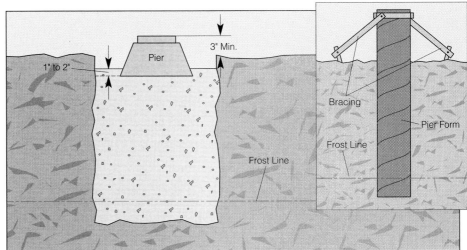

4 Fill the footing hole almost full with concrete; then place the precast pier blocks. If you're using a tube form, brace it if necessary and pour concrete to the desired height.

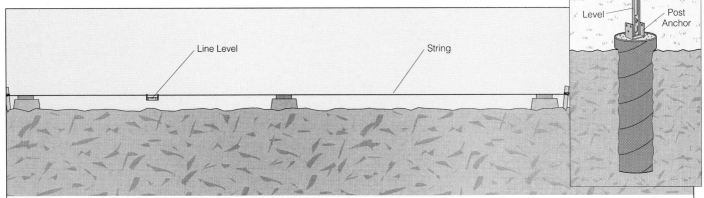

5 Adjust the height of the concrete piers with a line level and string. With a tube form, smooth the concrete; then insert and level a post anchor.

is to support the structure. Garage foundations are commonly constructed with concrete or concrete block. Foundation requirements for single- and double-car units are the same.

Monolithic Concrete Footing/Foundation

A monolithic concrete pour is one that's accomplished without using construction joints, or separation. The footing and foundation are poured as a single component.

In a monolithic design, the footing and foundation may be poured the same width, eliminating a lot of formwork. This procedure is practical only for a minimum-width footing in firm soil where the frost line is not deep. The trench is cut with vertical sides the width of the footing. No forming is required except for the foundation portion extending above the ground surface. (See page 30.)

Building a Concrete-Block Foundation

You might want to build a block foundation where the wall must be much more than about 8 inches high in sandy soil, for example, and you don't want to build a lot of formwork. Foundation walls constructed with Grade N, 8 x 8 x 16-inch concrete block are code-approved in most areas. The actual size of the block is $7\frac{5}{8}$ x $7\frac{5}{8}$ x $15\frac{5}{8}$ inches. Use hollow-core, load-bearing blocks and Type M or S mortar for foundation walls.

1 **Starting the Work.** Begin the block work by establishing the exact outside corners of the building. To accomplish this you might need to reattach the batter-board strings if you've removed them. Snap a chalk line along one of the footing walls. To lay out the block course, begin at one corner and place a block with the outside face flush with the chalk line. Continue placing blocks, without mortar, on the footing $\frac{3}{8}$ inch apart. This space is the preferred thickness

of the mortar joint, which added to the $15\frac{5}{8}$ -inch block, gives the full 16-inch dimension. You can make minor adjustments by slightly closing or opening the joints. Keep the joints under $\frac{1}{2}$ inch, however.

2 **Mixing Mortar.** Mix mortar in a wheelbarrow or concrete mixing tub, following the manufacturer's directions. You'll know the mortar is mixed properly when its texture is

like that of clay and it holds its shape when squeezed.

3 **Laying Corner Blocks.** To ensure a professional job, begin by laying the corners. Sweep the footing clean, and spread a full mortar bed for each block. Make the bed no thicker than 1 inch; a thicker bed doesn't hold the block weight well. If the foundation wall is one block high, lay two blocks as shown in the draw-

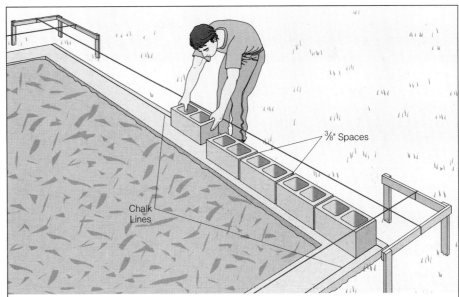

1 Establish the outside corners of the structure using batter boards and string, then snap a guide line for the first row of blocks. Dry-lay the blocks to establish correct spacing.

3/8" Spaces

Chalk Lines

2 Mix mortar until its texture is like that of clay.

3 For a one-course wall, lay two blocks for the corner.

ing. For a wall two blocks high, lay a third block for the second course lapping over the corner formed by the first two blocks. For a foundation wall higher than two blocks, lay additional blocks at the corners, lapping the joints in each course.

Low and high spots in the footing can cause major problems if not corrected. Trim the block using a cold chisel to fit high places. Fill in low spots with pieces of block and mortar. These precautions will keep the course level, avoiding dips and humps in the wall.

4 Laying the First Course. With the two- or three-block corners in place, you're ready to lay the first course. Pull a taut nylon string at block height from one corner to the next. Use a wood line block to hold the string in place. You can buy line blocks at the same place you bought the concrete block.

Butter one end of each block you lay before placing it. Press the buttered end to the previously laid block for the desired joint width as indicated by your dry run. Lay the block to the string, keeping the outside top corner edge of each block the same exact distance from the string.

5 Laying Subsequent Blocks. Lay a good bed of mortar on top of the block already set to provide a seat for the block you're about to set for a second course. Once you've positioned the new block properly, remove excess mortar from the face of the joint. Don't smear the block with mortar. Cut excess mortar squeezed from joints cleanly with the edge of your trowel.

6 Checking for Level. Frequently check your work with a spirit level along the length of the blocks and across the width. Use both 24- and 48-inch-size levels if possible. Check the width of the block the shorter level and the length, spanning several blocks, using the longer one.

7 Cutting Block. At certain points it may be necessary to cut the concrete block. Use a cold chisel and

4 To lay the concrete block, "butter" one end and, using a taut string as a guide, set each unit in a bed of mortar.

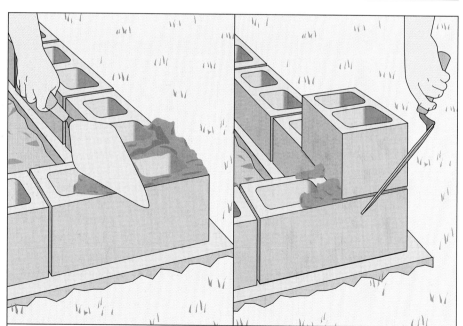

5 Apply a bed of mortar to the corner blocks as a seat for the next course. Remove mortar squeeze-out from the face of the block by cutting it with the edge of a trowel.

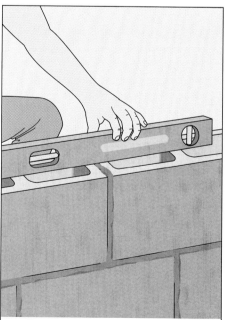

6 Check for level every few blocks across the length and width of the block.

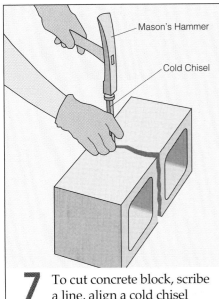

7 To cut concrete block, scribe a line, align a cold chisel with the line, and strike the chisel with a mason's hammer.

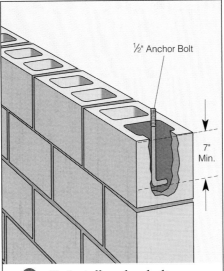

8 To install anchor bolts for the mudsills, fill block cavities with mortar and set the bolts a maximum of 72 in. apart.

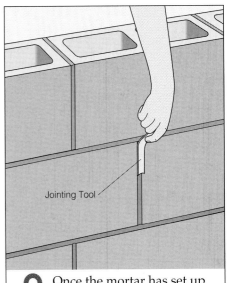

9 Once the mortar has set up but not hardened, tool the joints to make them uniform and ensure a good seal.

mason's hammer. Scribe a line at the appropriate place on the block. Align the chisel with the line, and strike the chisel firmly with the mason's hammer. The block should crack along the line.

8 **Installing Anchor Bolts.** The Uniform Building Code (UBC) requires foundation plates, or mudsills, be bolted to the foundation wall with anchor bolts or similar approved hardware. The anchor bolts should be at least ½ inch in diameter, embedded at least 7 inches into the concrete or masonry and spaced not more than 72 inches apart. A minimum of two bolts per sill piece is required, with one bolt located within 12 inches of each end. Plug the bottom of the block's core; place bolts in the center of the core; and fill it with mortar.

9 **Tooling the Joints.** Once the mortar has set for a while, press it with your thumb. If your thumbprint remains and no mortar sticks to your thumb, the joints are ready to be tooled. Smooth the joints with a jointing tool to ensure a good seal. You'll have some joint patching to do regardless of how carefully you work. It's best to patch while the mortar is still plastic. If you must patch after the mortar hardens, gouge out the joint about ½ inch, wet it, and patch it with fresh mortar.

Making a Concrete-Slab Foundation

Requirements for a concrete-slab foundation vary depending on climate, soil conditions, and the weight of the structure it must support. For garages and carports, the slab is typically about 4 inches thick, laid over a base of at least 4 inches of gravel or crushed rock. Spread the gravel evenly and tamp it. Crushed rock, gravel, and sand will shrink between 10 and 15 percent of its volume when compacted, so keep this in mind when ordering materials.

A plastic vapor barrier sandwiched between the gravel and concrete keeps subsurface moisture from seeping up through the slab. Six-mil-thick polyethylene provides an excellent barrier. Overlap seams in the plastic film 12 inches or more to ensure a good seal. It's usually a good idea to put down a layer of at least 1 inch of sand on top of the gravel so the plastic doesn't get punctured.

The slab perimeter has a thickened "turned down" footing to support the walls. In most cases the footing is 6 to 12 inches thick; check with your building department. With shallow footings,

the slab and footing can be made in one pour and only one set of forms is required. If the perimeter footing needs to be much deeper, you'll have to pour it separately, using the method described on page 30.

The slab is reinforced with 6 x 6-inch No. 10 wire mesh or a grid of ½-inch

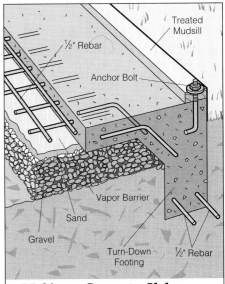

Making a Concrete-Slab Foundation. A concrete slab may be poured at the same time as a shallow turned-down footing. Gravel provides a good base. A vapor barrier prevents moisture migration.

rebar. The wire mesh is available in rolls 60 inches wide and 150 feet long. Overlap the seams at least 6 inches. Instead of using wire mesh or rebar in the slab, you can order fiber-reinforced concrete from the ready-mix company. This special concrete is more expensive, but it saves labor. Place rebar in the footings, as for a perimeter footing, even if you're using fiber-reinforced concrete.

1 Excavating the Slab and Footing.
Using batter boards and strings as a guide, excavate the slab area and the footing trench to the desired depths. If the slab is to be 4 inches thick and you're back-filling underneath it with 4 inches of gravel and 1 inch of sand, for example, you'd excavate the slab area to a depth of only 3 inches. The resulting slab surface would then be about 6 inches above ground level. The depth of the footing trench depends on climatic and soil conditions in your area and the size of the garage or carport.

2 Locating the Forms.
Now set up the batter-board strings to represent the outside face of the footing/slab, which also represents the inside face of the form boards. At each corner, drop a plumb line from the intersecting strings to the bottom of the trench and drive a 2x4 stake at this point. Using the plumb bob again, drive a nail into the top of the stake where the plumb bob touches it. Attach strings between the stakes. Using the strings as guides, drive 2x4 form stakes around the trench perimeter, spaced on 24-inch centers. The inside faces of the stakes should be away from the strings at a distance equal to the thickness of the form boards.

3 Attaching the Form Boards.
Attach two-by form boards to the stakes with double-headed nails. Make sure the stakes are on the outside of the boards and flush with or below their tops. As you attach the boards, level and adjust them for

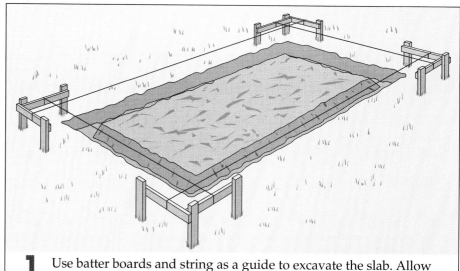

1 Use batter boards and string as a guide to excavate the slab. Allow for a minimum of 4 in. of gravel, 1 in. of sand, and 4 in. of concrete.

2 Use strings to determine the outside face of the slab, which is the inside face of the forms.

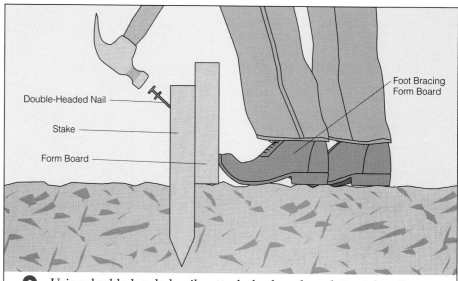

Double-Headed Nail

Foot Bracing Form Board

Stake

Form Board

3 Using double-headed nails, attach the form boards to stakes. Be sure the stakes are below the form's top surface.

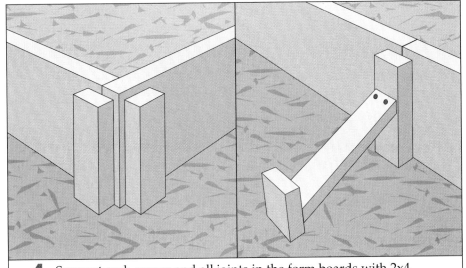

4 Support each corner and all joints in the form boards with 2x4 stakes—and braces where necessary.

height. Make sure each corner forms a 90-degree angle, using the 3-4-5 triangulation method described on page 25. After you've attached the boards, double-check your work by measuring opposite diagonals. If both diagonals are the same length, the forms are square.

4 **Bracing the Forms.** Use 2x4 stakes to brace the corners of the forms. If you must join two shorter boards to make one long one, brace the joint as shown.

Pouring the Concrete

1 **Using Isolation Joints.** If you're pouring a slab against an existing building or inside a foundation, use a fiber isolation joint. The material allows for different expansion and contraction rates. You can buy the ½-inch thick material from concrete supply stores.

2 **Preparing to Pour.** Backfill the excavation with 4 inches of gravel and tamp it firm. Cover the gravel with sand; then lay down the polyethylene vapor barrier. Place wire mesh

reinforcement or rebar if you're using it. The wire should sit in the top half of the slab, so use small stones or pieces of brick or concrete to raise the reinforcement about 2 inches above the plastic. Also position rebar in the footing if you're pouring a slab foundation. If the soil is dry, dampen it a day or two before the pour. Mist the area again just before you pour. Oil the inside of the forms to make them easier to remove after the concrete sets.

3 **Pouring and Spreading the Concrete.** Start as far back in the form as possible. Don't dump loads of concrete on top of each other; succeeding loads should be dumped against each other. Spread the concrete using a rake or hoe, compacting it gently into the footings if necessary. Using rake tines, pull up the reinforcing mesh as you spread the concrete to make sure there are no voids. Pour the concrete slightly above the forms to allow for settling.

4 **Screeding the Surface.** Use a long, straight 2x4 to screed, or level, the concrete. The screed should span the formwork, resting on top of the form boards. Starting at the back end of the pour, move the screed toward the front to strike off excess

Concrete-Block Foundation

Isolation-Joint Material

1 When you pour concrete against any structure, install a fiber isolation joint.

2 Backfill the excavated area with gravel, sand, a vapor barrier, wire mesh, and/or rebar.

3 Lift the wire mesh slightly to be sure concrete surrounds it without voids.

concrete. Move the board from side to side as you pull it toward you. Using a shovel, remove surplus concrete that piles up in front of the screed, and place the surplus in any low spots or in a wheelbarrow to be used later if needed (within 20 minutes).

5 **Floating the Concrete.** Tamp the concrete with a concrete tamper (available at rental centers),

then smooth it with a bullfloat. The bullfloat smooths the surface, removing the screed marks and causing the aggregate to work to the surface of the concrete.

Work the float at a 90-degree angle to the screed direction. Drop the handle down as you push the float over the surface. This lifts the front edge of the float to prevent "digging"

the concrete surface. Lift the handle to raise the rear edge as you pull the float back toward you. At the end of each stroke, lift the float and move it over to make another parallel stroke. Push and pull in this manner until you've worked the surface of the wet concrete smooth.

6 **Cutting Control Joints.** Use a groover tool with a minimum 1-inch blade to cut control joints in the slab. Control joints are commonly spaced at 10-foot intervals. Control joints help control cracking that may occur when the concrete shrinks or contracts due to the curing process and swings in temperature.

7 **Troweling.** After the bullfloating and jointing is complete and the concrete starts to set you can start troweling with a hand trowel or float. A steel trowel will produce a smooth surface suitable for a garage or carport floor. A wooden float produces a rougher, skidproof surface. Work the hand tool in a 180-degree arc over the concrete surface, keeping the blade nearly flat to produce a smooth surface.

4 Level, or screed, the concrete by striking off the excess with a straight 2x4.

5 Once you've screeded it, smooth the concrete with a bullfloat, a long-handled float.

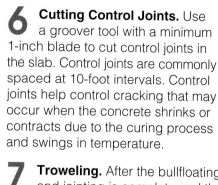

Control Joint

Controlled Crack

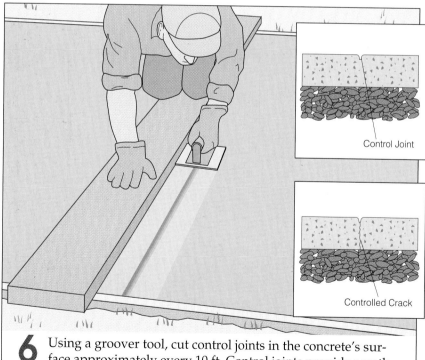

6 Using a groover tool, cut control joints in the concrete's surface approximately every 10 ft. Control joints provide a path for cracks, which are inevitable in any concrete slab, to follow.

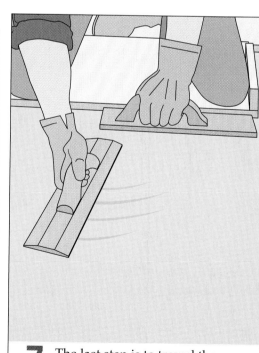

7 The last step is to trowel the surface with a wood float (rough texture) or steel trowel (smooth texture).

framing

Framing a Garage

There are three basic approaches to stick-building a one-story wall: tilt-up framing, built-in-place framing, and a combination of the two.

Tilt-up framing entails putting together all the pieces on the floor and lifting the wall into position as a complete unit. You'd normally place the assembled wall on top of a previously installed sill plate, which gives a double bottom plate, or lift the wall onto anchor bolts seated in the foundation. You'll need to have a helper handy, at least when it comes time to tilt up the stud walls.

You can also build the wall on the floor without the bottom plate, lift the wall into position on the anchored sill plate, and toenail each of the studs to the sill plate with four 12/2d common nails, two on each side. The garage door opening may be framed in place instead of framed horizontally on the floor and tilted into position.

You start a built-in-place wall by toenailing the corner posts to the sill plate and temporarily bracing them plumb. You nail the top plate in place and then fill in the studs and the framed openings for doors and windows. We'll cover building with the tilt-up method here.

Before you start framing the walls, determine the location and size of the rough openings for doors and windows. Frame each long wall to equal the overall length of the building, then fit the two shorter walls between them. To avoid framing mistakes during construction, make an elevation drawing of each wall, showing the sizes and spacing of various framing members.

1 Sealing the Mudsills. Use a foam or fiberglass sill gasket to seal the sill where it meets the foundation. This seal isn't absolutely necessary unless you're going to insulate the garage, but it helps seal out insects and air infiltration, so it's a good idea for attached garages.

2 Setting the Mudsills. Select straight 16-foot or longer pressure-treated two-bys as the mudsills for long walls. For an 8-inch-wide concrete-block stem wall, use 2x8s. For a poured stem wall, use lumber that fits its width. For a slab, use lumber the same dimension at the framing lumber. Square the end cuts to ensure that butt joints and corners fit tightly. Place the sill piece against the anchor bolts with one cut end flush with an outside wall. Use a framing square to align the lines from each anchor bolt across the mudsill. Measure the distance from the outside edge of the foundation to the center of the bolt. Transfer this measurement to the mudsill to mark the center of the bolt hole, and drill ½-inch-diameter holes in the sill. The oversize hole will enable you to make slight adjustments.

Lower the mudsills over the anchor bolts; then place wide washers and the appropriate-size nuts over the bolts. Turn the nuts finger-tight and check the corners. Make any necessary adjustments; then tighten the bolts with an open-end or socket wrench.

3 Marking the Plates. Once the mudsills are installed, start at a long side wall and lay the bottom plate the full length of the wall. Lay the top plate beside the bottom plate, and make both plates the same length. Measure and mark both members for stud placement at the same time. Mark the studs for the corner post as shown. Next, for 16-inch stud spacing using 2x4s, measure in 15¼ inches from the left end, mark a line, and place an X on the right side of the mark. Proceed to mark off every 16 inches to the opposite end. Place an X on the right side of each mark. Now go back and, with a combination or framing square, square up each mark you made, measure 1½ inches across

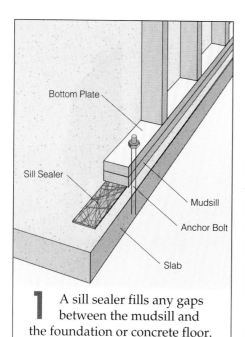

1 A sill sealer fills any gaps between the mudsill and the foundation or concrete floor.

2 Use a square to mark the anchor-bolt locations on the mudsill for 1-in. drill holes.

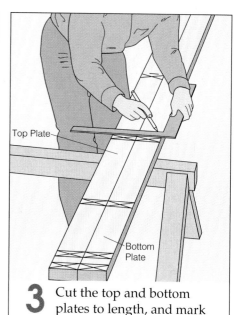

3 Cut the top and bottom plates to length, and mark the locations of all studs.

the X mark, and draw another squared line. This gives you an exact outline for the placement of each stud.

For 24-inch spacing using 2x6s, measure in from the end 23¼ inches, and proceed with the layout following the same procedure as above using 24-inch measurements.

Headers, king studs, jack studs, and cripple studs make up the framing components for openings. Determine the location of king studs, jack studs, headers, and cripples, and mark the appropriate plate for these pieces— top plate for king studs and headers; bottom plate for king studs, jack studs, and cripples under windows.

4 **Assembling the Wall.** Once you've marked the plates, place the bottom plate into position over the mudsill. Note where the anchor bolts protrude into the bottom plate. Measure and mark these spots; then drill or chop out enough wood to allow the plate to clear the bolts. Now frame the corner posts for the long walls as shown. For blocking, use three spacer blocks about 12 inches long. Locate the blocks flush with the post ends and at the midpoint. Face-nail the blocks to a stud with three 8d nails, then face-nail the opposite stud to the blocks, also with three

8d nails. If you precut the studs, cut them to a height that will give you a 96-inch finished ceiling. Remember that the mudsill, bottom plate, and double top plate add up to 6 inches. Take into account the height of the foundation wall, if any. Lay out the rest of the studs at the marked positions between the bottom and top plates. Face-nail each stud through the plates with two 16d nails at each plate.

5 **Framing Door and Window Openings.** Locate the door and window headers the same height from the floor by using double 2x12s for all openings. Sandwich ½-inch plywood or oriented-strand-board (OSB) panels between the two header members of wide openings for added strength. King studs are regular-length studs to which header members are attached. Face-nail the stud to the header with four 16d nails. Face-nail the king studs through bottom and top plates with two 16d nails. King studs may or may not be located at on-center positions. Jack studs are also called trimmer studs and jamb studs. Use these to support the ends of a header. Face-nail the trimmer to the king stud with 10d nails spaced 16 inches apart. Cripple studs are short studs used as support in window openings. Place cripples at on-center positions

to continue the proper stud spacing. Nail the cripples through the bottom plate and through the sill with two 16d nails at each position.

Exterior passage doors are generally 32, 34, or 36 inches wide by 80 inches high. As a rule of thumb, make the rough opening 2½ inches wider than the door, assuming a ¾ inch jamb, and 1½ inches higher than the door when not using a threshold. Prehung doors fit directly into the rough opening, so make sure the opening is the right size. Either measure the door unit or have it on site before framing the opening to make certain you get it right.

Windows are available in many standard sizes and styles. Manufacturers often provide rough-opening specifications, but generally, make the rough opening ½ inch wider than the window unit width and ¾ inch higher than the unit height.

6 **Lifting the Wall into Position.** Lift the framed side wall and place it on the mudsill with the assistance of one or two helpers. Flush the outside edges of the bottom plate with the mudsill; tack the plate in place; and plumb the wall using temporary braces. Face-nail the bottom plate to the sill plate between each stud with two 10d nails.

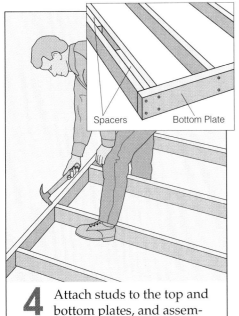
Spacers   Bottom Plate

4 Attach studs to the top and bottom plates, and assemble the corner posts.

King Studs
2x12 Header
Bracing
Sill
Trimmer Studs
Cripple Stud

5 Frame window and door openings with king studs, trimmer studs, cripple studs, and headers. The bottom plate that spans the door opening will be cut away at a later point.

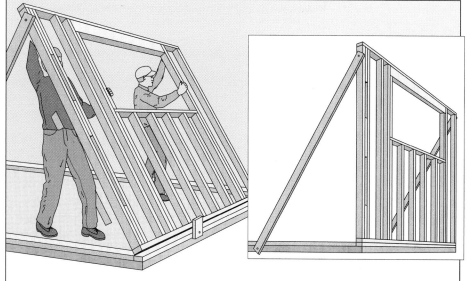

6 With a helper or two, tilt the wall section into place, plumb it, brace it in position, and nail it to the mudsill.

7 Lift the other walls into position, and nail them together.

7 **Building and Erecting the Remaining Walls.** Frame, lift, plumb, and brace the opposite side wall, then the back wall. When you lay out the back wall first stud, measure 11¼ inches to account for the side wall corner studs. Connect the three walls at the corners by driving 16d nails at 12-inch intervals through the end studs of the end walls into the corner posts of the first two sidewalls.

8 **Framing the Garage Door Opening.** Garage doors are available in 8-, 9-, 10-, 12-, 14-, 16-, 17-, and 18-foot widths and in 78-, 84-, and 96-inch heights. Select the garage door before framing so you can follow the door manufacturer's requirements. To ensure adequate overhead space for the door and related equipment, such as tracks, springs, motor drive, and the like, plan for the space in advance. Work

out the head and jamb details to suit the door. If the header is located in a gable end wall, it's not required to carry roof and ceiling loads and may be a double 2x10 for openings up to 12 feet or double 2x8s for openings up to 10 feet. Door openings in a side wall require headers of sufficient size to support ceiling and roof loads because the side wall is a load-bearing wall.

9 **Adding Cap Plates.** To complete the framing, add the cap plates, which must be the same size as the top plates. Make the top of the wall as straight as possible before installing the cap. Use a taut gauge string and ¾-inch-thick blocks as shown. Tack a block to the side of the top plate near each end of the wall. Drive a 16d nail halfway into the plate near the block. Pull a taut nylon string from nail to nail over the top of the blocks. Insert a ¾-inch block between the string and plate at different places along the plate to determine whether the plate is straight. If the plate's not straight, nail temporary braces to the stud immediately under the top plate, and force the wall into alignment. Nail the bottom of the brace to a stake. With the top plate aligned, nail down the cap with 10d nails staggered 16 inches apart. Offset butt joints in the top plate and

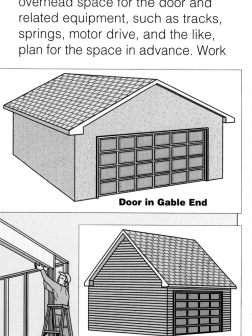

Door in Gable End

Door in Eave End

8 Garage-door openings require double jack studs and 2x6 jambs. A double 2x12 header is generally used, but a smaller header may be used if the door is on the gable end of the garage.

cap over wall studs and lap them at intersecting walls and corners.

10 Installing Sheathing.
Provide permanent bracing with let-in bracing or structural-panel sheathing. Here we'll use panels. Use wood structural-panel sheathing (CDX plywood or OSB) with a thickness of $7/16$ inch for studs on 16-inch centers and $5/8$ inch for studs spaced 24 inches. Orient the panels in a horizontal or vertical position, and nail them to the studs with 6d common nails spaced 6 inches at the edges and 12 inches at intermediate supports. Leave about $1/8$-inch gaps between the panels for expansion and stagger the joints. Install the panels flush with the top and sides of the walls, and overlap the foundation by at least $1/2$ inch, up to $2 1/2$ inches. Snap a level chalk line across the foundation face as a guide for aligning the bottom edges of the panels. You can either sheathe right over door and window openings and cut them out later or cut the plywood before you nail it up. If you want a rustic treatment for your garage, you can use textured plywood with shiplap edges or boards and battens to serve as the sheathing and siding at the same time.

Building a Carport

The carports shown are open post-and-pier-type structures. Because of the minimum number of bearing points and long spans, precise fits at butt ends and joints are important. Make sure the posts are securely anchored at the base and top. Use at least 4x4 pressure-treated wood posts (4x6 posts for a flat roof used as a deck) or 4-inch steel columns for a one-car structure. Consult your local building department for larger structures.

The header of the open carport joining the wall of the house may be supported by columns at the wall or the house wall itself. To use a masonry wall as support, install a 2x6 or larger ledger to run the full length of the carport using lag screws secured to expansion sleeves fitted into holes drilled every 24 inches in the masonry. Insert sleeves in holes drilled in the brick or block. Do not install at mortar joints. Attach rafters to the ledger with adjustable joist hangers.

For a frame wall, attach a ledger running the length of the carport and secured to the house framing with $3/16$-inch lag screws long enough to penetrate the framing at least $2 1/2$ inches. Secure the rafters to the ledger as above with hanger hardware. Panel

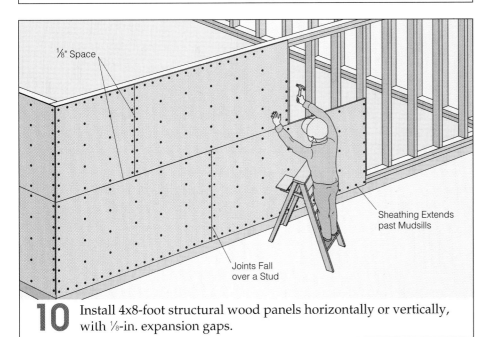

Illustrations (top row): B Laps A — A, B; Butt Plates over a Stud; Cap Laps Top Plate

9 Align the top plate on all walls using a guide block and string, and nail on the cap plate with 10d nails. Lap corners and intersections.

Labels: Sides Removed for Clarity; Hand-Held Block; String; Stand-off Block

10 Install 4x8-foot structural wood panels horizontally or vertically, with $1/8$-in. expansion gaps.

Labels: $1/8$" Space; Sheathing Extends past Mudsills; Joints Fall over a Stud

5 Framing

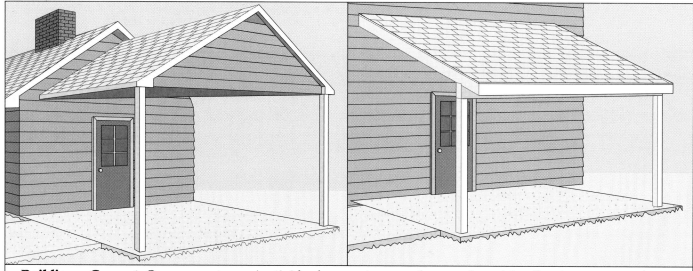

Building a Carport. Open carports require rigid columns, strong anchors, and precision fits. A carport may have a gable roof (left) or a shed roof (right).

siding and synthetic siding materials need not be removed.

1 Making Built-up Headers. Choose the kind of header you want to use. If you decide on a built-up header, build it by nailing together two pieces of two-by lumber such as 2x10s. In long spans, such as might be required in a 24-foot-long carport, stagger the joints so they fall directly over intermediate supports. Nail the header from one side with 10d nails, two at the ends and staggered along the length 16 inches apart.

2 Bracing the Posts. Put the posts in place on their pedestals or bases. Temporary braces hold the posts in position during construction. Brace the posts on two sides with rigid temporary braces like 2x4s to ensure

they remain plumb. For wood posts, nail the braces near the top and secure the bottom of the braces to stout stakes. For a steel post, clamp a wood block to the post and nail the braces to the block at the top and to stakes at the bottom.

Permanent bracing of the post to the header is usually not necessary for attached units because the racking forces are resisted by the roof framing that's joined to the house. Permanent braces are recommended at the corners of detached open units. Attach a 16- to 24-inch brace to the

header and post at a 45-degree angle. Install two braces at each corner. Use a minimum ¼-inch-thick by 2-inch-wide steel strap for the brace. Attach the straps to wood with ³⁄₁₆ x 2¼-inch lag screws. Bolt them to steel posts with ¼-inch bolts.

3 Installing the Headers. Before you build a roof over the carport you'll need to install headers, which will form the structural support for the roof. Determine the size header you'll need. (See "Common Header Sizes," opposite.) If you're using steel posts, you'll find a steel plate attached to the

1 Make a built-up header by nailing together two-by lumber with 10d nails.

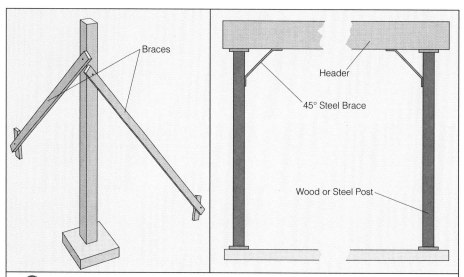

Braces

Header

45° Steel Brace

Wood or Steel Post

Joints Staggered over Supports

2 Plumb and brace carport posts before starting header and roof construction. Leave temporary braces in place until framing is complete. For an unattached carport, brace the structure with permanent steel braces.

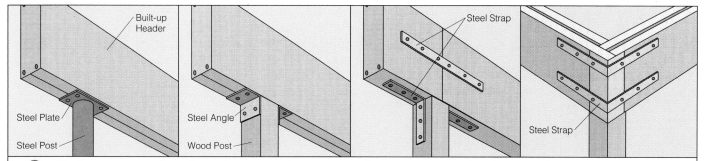

Built-up Header

Steel Plate

Steel Post

Steel Angle

Wood Post

Steel Strap

Steel Strap

3 Use lag screws and steel attachment hardware to attach carport posts to headers. Reinforce joints and corners with steel strapping.

top of each post through which you drive screws to attach the header. For wood posts, attach steel angles to the post and header. For both kinds of posts use ³⁄₁₆-inch lag screws long enough to penetrate the header 2 inches or more. If you must join sections of a solid header, butt them and tie the joint over a post with steel strapping. Tie the header corners using metal strapping, secured with ³⁄₁₆ x 1³⁄₄-inch lag screws. Lap the corner of a built-up header as shown.

Common Header Sizes

The greater the span of a header, the stronger the header must be. When its length is doubled, for example, the safe carrying load of a given-size header is reduced by three-quarters and not one-half as you might expect. Header strength can be increased by using a stronger material or a thicker or wider piece of the same material. You can also make a flitch beam for added strength by sandwiching plywood with two-by lumber. Here are some common header sizes and the spans they can safely handle.

Header Size	Maximum Span
Double 2x6	6 feet
Double 2x8	8 feet
Double 2x10	10 feet
Double 2x12	12 feet

Choosing Header Stock

Your header may be a built-up solid wood beam, an engineered lumber beam, or a wood I-beam. Built-up and engineered lumber headers exposed to the weather and not properly protected by a roof, eave overhang, or protective covering must be pressure-treated to resist insect infestation and decay caused by moisture.

Built-up Solid Beam. This is the least costly kind of header, and it is easily made. (See Step 1 on page 44.) The grain of the individual lumber pieces run differently, giving the beam greater stability.

Engineered Lumber. These manufactured structural members are capable of spanning long distances and supporting heavy loads. Engineered lumber includes.

■ Glue-laminated beams, fabricated by bonding several layers of same-size boards, such as 2x4s and 2x6s, together, and made with a slight crown that is always turned up.

■ LVL beams, made by bonding pine veneer with exterior adhesives. The beams are available in many sizes and lengths up to 26 feet. LVL will not warp, twist, or shrink and is easy to nail and saw.

■ Beams made from parallel-strand strips of lumber, known by the trademark Parallam.

I-beams. I-beams have top and bottom flanges made from kiln-dried lumber in nominal sizes: 2x2, 2x3, and 2x4. The 2x4 flanges may be doubled for greater load-bearing capacity. The web, or center member, may be ³⁄₈- or ⁵⁄₈-inch CDX plywood or OSB. The beams are available in various depths and in lengths up to 26 feet. I-beams are manufactured by a number of companies under different trade names.

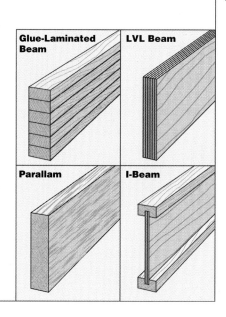

Glue-Laminated Beam

LVL Beam

Parallam

I-Beam

Framing the Roof

Most garages and carports are built with either a gable roof or a shed roof. Rafter and ceiling joist materials for site-built roofs are commonly 2x6 lumber. Roof trusses are discussed on pages 74 to 76.

Roof framing takes more skill than wall framing because you need to cut rafter ends at an angle and notch them to fit over the top plates of the walls. Determine the pitch or slope of the roof before you start. Steep roofs require longer rafters but are better suited to cold climates where the roof must be able to shed heavy snow loads. Shallower roofs are acceptable in warm climates.

Roof pitch is expressed as the ratio of the rafter's total vertical rise to the span of the roof. A 24-foot wide garage, for example, with a gable roof that rises

10 feet in the middle has a 10/24, or 5/12, pitch. The more commonly used roof slope is expressed as the rafter's vertical rise in inches per 12 inches of horizontal run and is the ratio between the roof's total rise and total run. The total run is one-half the width of the garage. Once you know the total run and rise, you can calculate the slope, and vice versa. If the rafter rises 5 inches for every 12 inches of run, for example, the slope is 5 in 12. A 5-in-12 roof on a 20-foot-wide garage rises 50 inches. The roof with a 5/12 *pitch* has a *slope* of 10 in 12.

A 3-in-12 slope is the minimum recommended for installing asphalt or wood shingles; for shallower slopes use asphalt roll roofing with sealed joints. A slope of 6 in 12 or steeper is recommended in areas subject to heavy snow loads. After you've determined the roof style and slope you want, decide how much overhang to

allow at the eaves and gable ends. A common overhang is 16 or 18 inches. These dimensions will determine the overall length of the rafters.

It's a good idea to build scaffolding or a catwalk at each side of the structure at a height that puts you at the top of the plate or header to help in roof framing, sheathing, and shingling. Standard steel scaffolding is available at many equipment rental stores. The rental can be expensive. The alter-native is to use 2x4 horizontal braces secured to the wall posts or wall studs at 48-inch intervals and supported by 2x4 uprights extended from the ground to provide a suitable rack for a 2x8 or 2x10 plank catwalk. Nail the braces and the plank securely to support workers' weight.

Preparing the Rafters

1 **Calculating Rough Rafter Lengths.** You'll need to know approximate rafter lengths when you order lumber. You can use your framing square to estimate this length. Let the blade of the square represent the total run and the tongue represent the total rise. Using a scale of 1 inch = 1 foot, measure the distance from the blade to the tongue to find the rough length of the rafter. Add in any eave overhang as extra length on the blade before you do your calculations.

2 **Laying Out the Ridge Cut.** Lay a straight piece of rafter stock across two sawhorses. Sight down the edge of the rafter and position yourself so that you're on the crowned side.

Let's say you want to lay out a roof with an 8-in-12 slope. Lay the square on the left end of the stock. Hold the square's tongue in your left hand and its blade in your right. Pivot the square until the edge of the stock nearer you aligns with the unit rise mark (8 inches in this example) on the outside of the tongue and the 12-inch mark on the outside of the blade. Mark along the outside edge of the tongue for the plumb cut at

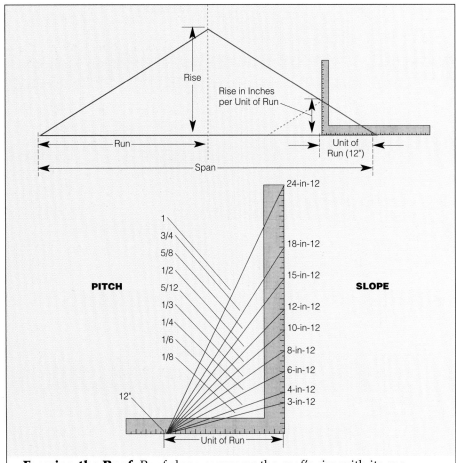

Framing the Roof. Roof slope compares the roof's rise with its run, which is half the span. Pitch is the ratio of the roof's rise to its span.

the ridge. You'll use this mark as the reference line for stepping off full 12-inch units.

3 Stepping Off the Rafter and Cutting the Bird's Mouth.
Working with the same 8-in-12 slope,

start to step off the rafter. Continue stepping off to your right by marking the stock on the outside of the blade and shifting the square until the outside of the tongue aligns with that mark. Perform this step a total of 12 times.

On the last step, mark a plumb line along the outside of the tongue. This plumb line, called the building line, should be directly above the outside of the cap plate.

The bird's mouth of the rafter is a combination level cut and plumb cut. The level cut rests on the top plate of the wall; the plumb cut fits snugly against the outside edge of the cap plate. Form the bird's mouth by measuring 1½ inches up the building line and drawing a perpendicular line to the inside edge of the rafter. Use a handsaw to cut the bird's mouth.

4 Measuring the Tail.
The rafter tail length is measured as a level dimension. To lay out the tail, simply add in the necessary amount of run (18 inches in this case—see the drawing), measuring from the plumb line of the bird's mouth. The tail cut is at the end of the rafter overhang and may be a plumb cut, square cut, or combination of cuts, depending on fascia treatment.

5 Shortening the Common Rafter for the Ridge.
The length of the rafter has been calculated to the center of the ridge line. You must therefore shorten the rafter to accommodate the ridgeboard. Measure back at a right angle from the ridge line a distance of one-half the thickness of the ridgeboard. Mark another plumb line at this point to arrive at the final length of the rafter.

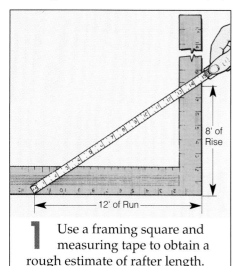

1 Use a framing square and measuring tape to obtain a rough estimate of rafter length.

(labeled: 8' of Rise, 12' of Run)

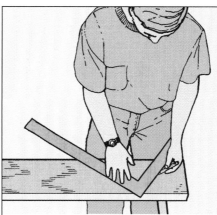

2 Align the tongue with the rise and the blade with the run to mark the ridge cut.

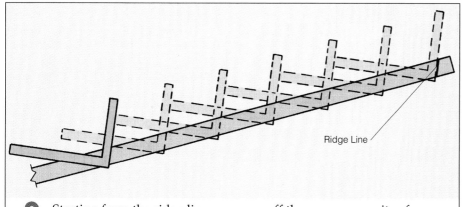

3 Starting from the ridge line, measure off the necessary units of run to come to the building line.

(labeled: Ridge Line)

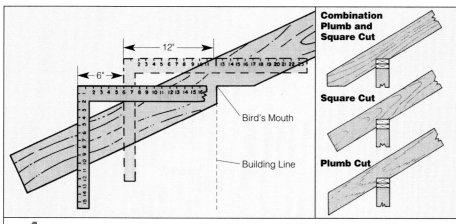

4 Measure the rafter tail horizontally from the building line. The rafter end may be cut in any number of ways.

(labeled: Combination Plumb and Square Cut, Square Cut, Plumb Cut, Bird's Mouth, Building Line, 12", 6")

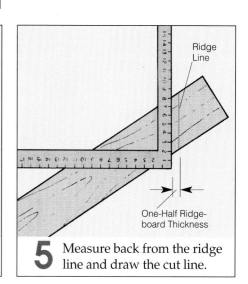

5 Measure back from the ridge line and draw the cut line.

(labeled: Ridge Line, One-Half Ridgeboard Thickness)

Installing the Ridgeboard

1 Setting Ceiling Joists and Ties.
In stick construction you place the ceiling joists and rafters parallel at the plate and face-nail them together with three or more 16d nails. Attach the ceiling joists prior to installing the rafters, and cut the ends of the joists to fit the slope of the rafters at the plate. To do this, measure the height of a rafter as it would sit on the top plate, at the end of the bird's mouth and along the plumb line. Transfer this measurement to the end of the ceiling joist. Align the framing square with the top edge of the ceiling joist, with the tongue showing the unit rise and the blade showing the unit run. Slide the

square until the blade intersects the rafter-height mark, and pencil a mark along the blade. Cut the joist along the mark; then toenail the joist to the top plate with three 10d nails.

To make the joists rigid and level, tie them together with a 2x6 installed perpendicular across the top of the joists in the center of the span and fastened at each joist with two 16d nails.

2 Making a Ridgeboard Splice.
The ridgeboard may be a one-by or two-by. Use a width to allow full contact with the plumb cut of the rafter. Size the ridgeboard to fit the length of the garage or carport plus the gable overhang at each end. To span the full length of the building, you may have to join two boards, which creates a butt joint. To make the joint strong, cut an angle splice as shown in the drawing. Lay out the ridgeboard so the splice will fall between rafters. Scab the splice with ½-inch plywood or OSB fastened with 6d nails. Drop the scab slightly below the top of the ridge to clear the sheathing.

3 Raising the Ridgeboard. Lay the ridgeboard flat and perpendicular across the ceiling joists, centered in the structure. Mark the rafter layout in the same manner as you marked the stud layout. Allow for the gable-end overhang. Cut four rafters and place two near each end of the ridgeboard, one on each side. Face-nail the ridgeboard to one rafter on each end with three 16d nails.

While a helper lifts the ridgeboard, tack the two rafters at the plate with 8d nails. Install a temporary 2x4 support post under the ridgeboard near the center. Butt the opposite two rafters against the ridge; tack them at the plates; then face-nail them through the ridgeboard at an angle with three 16d nails.

Check the ridgeboard for level, and complete nailing the four rafters at the plates. Install the remaining rafters in pairs. Toenail the rafters to the wall plate with three 8d nails and face-nail them to the ceiling joists with a minimum of three 16d nails. You can also use metal hurricane ties to secure the rafters.

4 Installing Sway Braces. Brace the ridgeboard near each end, 12 inches from the building's edge, with a 2x4 upright and a 2x4 diagonal cut at 45-degree angles to prevent roof sway.

1 Mark the ceiling joists with a rafter square and cut them. You'll face-nail rafters to the joists.

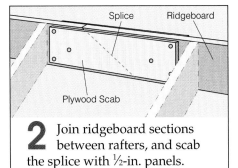

2 Join ridgeboard sections between rafters, and scab the splice with ½-in. panels.

3 Nail pairs of rafters at each end of the ridge while a helper supports the ridge.

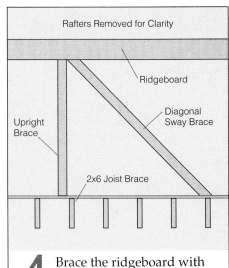

4 Brace the ridgeboard with 2x4s near each end, 12 in. from the building's edge.

Finishing the Framing

1 Building the Gable-End Overhang. The gable-end overhang is normally the same dimension as the eave overhang. Attach a set of barge rafters to the end of the ridge-board and to the end rafters with 2x4 blocks, called outriggers or lookouts, cut to the proper dimension to form the overhang. The roof sheathing will extend flush to the outside edge of the barge rafters.

2 Installing Fascia and Soffits. Use one-by or two-by subfascia to align the rafter tails at the eaves and provide a firm backer for the finish fascia. Drop the fascia boards as shown so as to not interfere with the sheathing's plane. Nail 1x4s, level with the bottom of the subfascia along the side walls, as a nailing base for the soffit. Nail 2x2s flush with the bottom of the end rafters as nailers for the gable soffits, and nail 1x8 fascia to the barge rafters. Install ⅜-inch

exterior plywood for the soffits. Use appropriate-size finishing nails to secure fascia and soffit materials.

3 Framing the Gable End. Cut the 2x4 gable-end short studs to fit between the top plate and the end rafters. Use a sliding bevel to transfer the proper angles to the tops of the studs. Toenail the studs to the top plate with four 8d nails directly over the end-wall studs, ensuring the same on-center spacing. Center the gable vent opening near the peak.

4 Venting the Roof. An enclosed attic space requires venting. Most building codes specify that the net free ventilating area be not less than $\frac{1}{150}$ of the ceiling area. An exception to this rule can be made if vents are at least 36 inches above vented eaves or cornices. In this case the ventilating area may be $\frac{1}{300}$ of the ceiling area. For a 24 x 24-foot structure having soffit vents, then, the required total net

vent area for the gable vent is $\frac{1}{300}$ of the ceiling area, or

24 feet x 28 feet = 672 square feet
672/300 = 2.24 square-foot vent area at each gable.

Cover vent openings with corrosion-resistant metal mesh with not less than ¼-inch openings. Protect vent openings against the entrance of rain and snow.

Continuous strip venting in the soffit provides the required ventilating area at the eaves. Also, 16 x 8-inch soffit vents may be installed at intervals in the soffit in lieu of the strip to provide the required soffit ventilation. Continuous ridge vents are efficient outlet vents and are acceptable alternatives to gable-end vents. The vent fits over a 3½-inch-wide slot in the sheathing at the ridge. Some vents eliminate the need for ridge cap shingles. Follow the manufacturer's installation instructions.

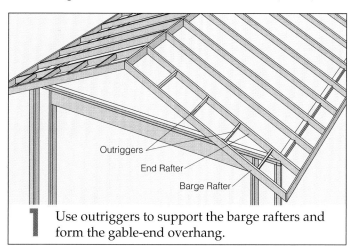

1 Use outriggers to support the barge rafters and form the gable-end overhang.

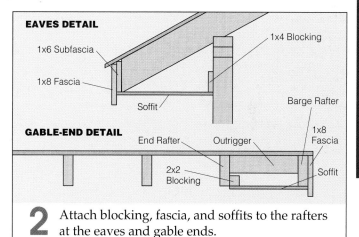

2 Attach blocking, fascia, and soffits to the rafters at the eaves and gable ends.

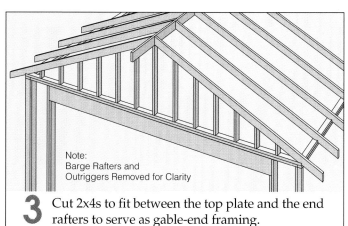

3 Cut 2x4s to fit between the top plate and the end rafters to serve as gable-end framing.

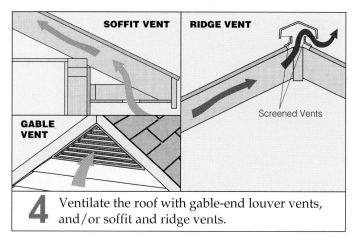

4 Ventilate the roof with gable-end louver vents, and/or soffit and ridge vents.

Building a Shed Roof

A shed roof carries a greater snow load because of its large flat surface, and it may require larger framing members. In areas with large snow loads, figure on 2x8s for a one-car structure. Give the roof at least enough slope (3 in 12) to ensure adequate water runoff.

1 Laying Out Rafters on Top Plates. Lay out and mark the rafter spacing on the top plates of the two supporting walls for the selected spacing of 16 or 24 inches. (See page 72 for how to build the slanting walls.) The first rafter and last rafter fit flush with the outside surface of the endwall top plates. Begin the layout on the left outside corner of the structure. Measure in from the end of the top plate—15¼ inches for 16-inch spacing—and mark a line. Place an X to the right of the line to indicate where you'll position the rafter. Mark off 16 inches, square off the line with a combination square, and place an X to the right of the line. Continue in this manner to the end of the plate. For 24-inch spacing, place the first mark 23¼ inches in from the plate's end and follow the same procedure as for 16-inch spacing, marking the plate every 24 inches.

2 Determining Rafter Size. You must decide on the size of the overhang you want before you can cut the rafters to fit. Make the eave overhang long enough to protect the headers and general carport area. A 16- or 18-inch overhang is usual. To determine the rafter length, measure between the outside surfaces of the top plates plus the overhang at the eaves or eave if the carport is attached.

The size of the rafter required depends primarily on the span and load. Flat roofs are generally required to carry a minimum uniform live load of 20 pounds per square foot (psf). A No. 2 2x8 made from southern pine will span about 12 feet under a 40 psf load—more than enough for a one-car carport. A No. 2 2x10 of the species will span about 16 feet. Figure on using 16-inch on-center spacing.

3 Laying Out and Cutting the Bird's Mouths. Cut a rafter to length, using an exceptionally straight piece. This will be the pattern for cutting the remaining rafters. Position the rafter across the headers with the correct overhang. Mark the rafter for the bird's-mouth cut with a square over the headers. Make the cuts 1½ inches deep to ensure a secure set. Cut the bird's mouth, test it, and mark the remaining rafter cuts using the pattern. Toenail the rafters to the headers using three 8d nails. Also use metal framing anchors for best results.

4 Installing Frieze Blocks. Install frieze blocks between the rafters flush with the outside of the header and in contact with the roof sheathing. Use a two-by cut to fit in the space and face-nail the blocks through each rafter with two 16d nails. Trim the rafter ends square, vertical (plumb), or a combination for a horizontal soffit. Determine the type of end-trimming you'll use when cutting the pattern rafter so you can make the end cuts when you cut the bird's mouths.

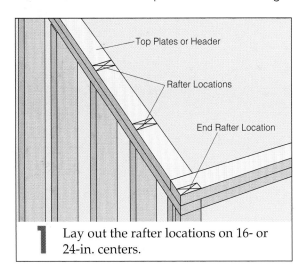

1 Lay out the rafter locations on 16- or 24-in. centers.

Top Plates or Header

Rafter Locations

End Rafter Location

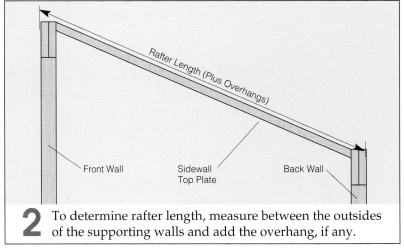

Rafter Length (Plus Overhangs)

Front Wall

Sidewall Top Plate

Back Wall

2 To determine rafter length, measure between the outsides of the supporting walls and add the overhang, if any.

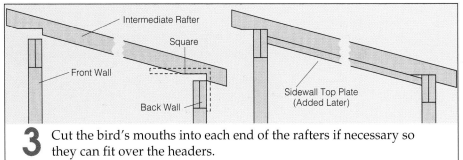

Intermediate Rafter

Square

Front Wall

Back Wall

Sidewall Top Plate (Added Later)

3 Cut the bird's mouths into each end of the rafters if necessary so they can fit over the headers.

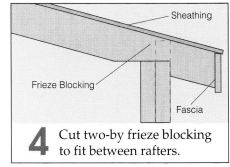

Sheathing

Frieze Blocking

Fascia

4 Cut two-by frieze blocking to fit between rafters.

finishing up

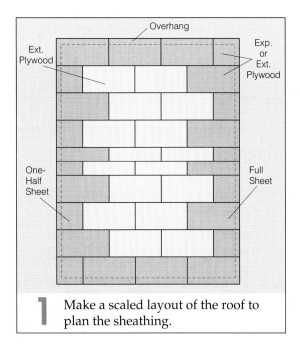

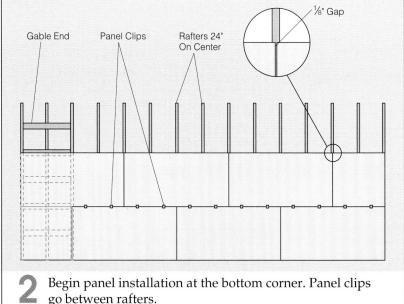

1 Make a scaled layout of the roof to plan the sheathing.

2 Begin panel installation at the bottom corner. Panel clips go between rafters.

Roof Sheathing

APA-The Engineered Wood Association rates plywood and oriented-strand board (OSB) panels for both roofing and flooring applications, and marks the panels with a span rating. Plywood panels with a 24/0 marking, for example, are adequate for rafters spaced 24 inches on center—but not for floors. APA-rated ½-inch plywood or OSB are suitable for either 24- or 16-inch-on-center rafters.

Use APA-rated Exposure 1 roof sheathing where the soffit is enclosed. For open soffits, use panels marked Exterior or Exposure 1 of the appropriate grade to permit painting or staining. You can also use ½- or ⅝-inch textured plywood with the textured side down for an attractive open soffit.

Installing Roof Sheathing

1 **Making the Sheathing Layout.** Draw a scaled sheathing layout for the entire roof on paper, showing panel sizes, placement, and number of panels; graph paper is easiest to use. Plan any panel cutting on one side so the cut-off portions can be used on the opposite side. You can start at the eave with a full panel, provided you don't end up at the top having to use a strip less than 16 inches wide. A narrow strip may

be too weak to support a person or provide a solid backing for the roofing. Trim the panels of the first row to adjust the width of the last row. Stagger the panels in succeeding rows so the ends fall on different framing members. The sketch will reveal the number of panels required over open soffits; use the appropriate grade panels over these areas.

2 **Installing the Panels.** Begin panel installation at a bottom corner of the roof, placing the long side perpendicular to the rafters and positioning the end joint over the center of a rafter. Stagger the panels by at least one rafter. Use H panel clips on ⅜-inch-thick panels installed on 24-inch-on-center rafters. Locate clips at mid-point between the rafters. Make the panel edges flush with rafter ends and the edges of barge rafters.

Fasten each panel using 8d common, spiral-threaded, or ring-shank nails. Space nails 6 inches apart along panel ends and 12 inches at intermediate supports. Leave a ⅛-inch space between panels for expansion. Start the second course with a half (4 x 4-foot) panel.

Use caution: The greater the roof slope, the more hazardous the job. On steep roofs, nail down 2x4 cleats

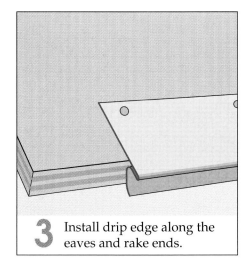

3 Install drip edge along the eaves and rake ends.

for footing support as you work up the roof.

3 **Installing the Drip Edge.** The drip edge, or drip cap, is a molded metal strip that fits the edges of the entire roof, both eaves and rakes, to divert water run-off. The edge comes in 10-foot lengths. Install the drip edge with ½-inch roofing nails (smaller for open soffits) along the eaves before applying the roofing felt to allow the roofing felt to overlap it. At the rake ends, install the drip edge over the felt.

4 **Laying Roofing Felt.** Asphalt-impregnated roofing felt is required as an underlayment under asphalt shingles. Attach the felt with staples or corrosion-resistant roofing

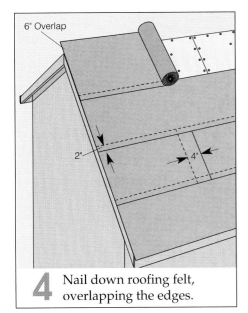

4 Nail down roofing felt, overlapping the edges.

Finished Roofing Materials

Depending on the slope of your roof, you'll use asphalt shingles or roll roofing. For roofs with a 4-in-12 or higher slope you can use three-tab or architectural-style asphalt shingles. Architectural shingles are thicker than conventional shingles and mimic the look of slate or wood shakes. Ideally, you'll try to match what you have on your house. For slopes less than 4-in-12, use roll roofing to prevent leakage.

Installing Shingles

Three-tab strip shingles are available in self-sealing asphalt and fiberglass bases. The shingle size most commonly used is 36 inches wide and 12 inches long, installed with 5 inches exposed to the weather. Approximate weight per square, or 100 square feet, is 215 pounds, with 66 shingles to the square in three separate bundles.

While roofers often have their own methods of applying strip shingles, our discussion will cover the 6-inch, 5-inch, and 4-inch trim methods with a 5-inch exposure. If you're installing architectural-type shingles, follow the manufacturer's instructions to achieve the proper look.

1 **Applying the Starter Strip.** The starter strip can be either a row of shingles trimmed to the manufacturer's specifications, a strip of mineral surface roll roofing at least 7 inches wide, or a course of shingles turned so the tabs face up the roof. The starter strip protects the roof by covering the spaces under the cutouts and joints of the first course of shingles. Extend the strip beyond the drip edge at the rake and eave by ¼ to ⅜ inch.

If you use trimmed or upside-down shingles, cut 6 inches from the end of the first shingle in the starter strip to ensure that the cutouts of the first course won't fall over the starter strip joints. Nail along a line parallel to the eave and about 4 inches above it. Place nails so they won't be exposed under the cutouts of the first course.

You might use 36-inch-wide roll roofing as a starter strip, to protect against ice damming in a cold climate. Establish an overhang of ¼ to ⅜ inch beyond the drip edge, and nail the roll roofing 4 inches up from the eave, with nails spaced 12 inches apart.

2 **Laying the Courses.** Keep the cutouts in a straight line as you work up the roof. Measuring from the edge of the roof and snapping chalk lines to guide every few courses will help you keep the shingles aligned. Begin the first course with a full-length shingle. On most of the remaining courses you'll trim a little off the first shingle to conform to the method of installation selected.

Depending on the length of your roof and how the shingles fit it, you'll use the 6-inch, 5-inch, or 4-inch method,

nails long enough to penetrate sheathing ¾ inch or through the sheathing thickness, whichever is less. In general, roof slope dictates the method of felt installation. In temperate climates, apply one layer of 15-pound felt on roofs having a 4-in-12 slope or greater. Lap the felt at least 2 inches horizontally and 4 inches vertically to shed water. Overlap the ridge by at least 6 inches.

On roofs having a 2-in-12 to less than 4-in-12 slope, start with a 19-inch-wide sheet at the eaves. Lay a 36-inch-wide sheet over the first, then lap each subsequent sheet 19 inches horizontally and 12 inches vertically. This layout, in effect, provides a double layer of felt.

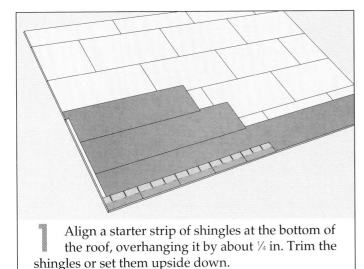

1 Align a starter strip of shingles at the bottom of the roof, overhanging it by about ¼ in. Trim the shingles or set them upside down.

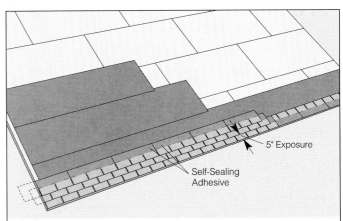

2 Start the first course with a full shingle, then trim the other courses according to the method you choose. Follow chalk lines every few courses.

Installing Flashing

Install flashing where the roof of an attached structure joins the house. All metal flashing must be at least 26-gauge (0.019-inch, or 0.48mm) corrosion-resistant coil stock. For a gable roof against a vertical side wall, you'll weave metal step flashing with the roof shingles as you install the shingles. The step-flashing pieces are rectangular, usually 10 inches long and 2 inches wider than the exposed face of the roofing shingles. Roofing shingles with a 5-inch exposure, for example, require 10 x 7-inch step flashing. Fold the 10-inch length in half so that it can extend 5 inches onto the roof deck and 5 inches up the wall.

Begin flashing installation by placing a section over the end of the roofing starter strip. Position the flashing so that it will be completely covered by the tab of the end shingle in the first course of roofing shingles. Use two nails to secure the horizontal arm of the flashing to the roof. Don't secure the flashing to the wall because settling on the garage/carport roof could damage this critical seal.

Apply the first course of roofing shingles. Then place the second piece of flashing over the end shingle in the first course of roofing shingles. Position the flashing shingle 5 inches up from the butt so that the flashing shingle will be completely covered by the tab of the end shingle in the second course of roofing shingles. Again, fasten the horizontal arm of the flashing to the roof. Apply the second course of roofing shingles. The end is flashed as in the preceding courses and so on to the ridge. Because the flashing is 7 inches wide and the roofing shingles are laid with a 5-inch exposure, each flashing section will overlap by 2 inches the one on the course below.

For a shed roof against a vertical wall, you'll lay shingles up the roof until a course must be trimmed to fit the base of the vertical wall. The last, trimmed course must be at least 8 inches wide, so it may be necessary to adjust the exposure of the preceding two courses to achieve this dimension. Check your spacing when you come to these courses.

Install a continuous piece of 26-gauge metal flashing over the last shingle course. Fold the flashing strip so that it will extend a minimum 5 inches up the wall and 4 inches onto the last course of shingles. Embed the flashing strip in asphalt plastic cement and nail it to the roof. Do not nail the flashing to the wall. Apply an additional row of shingles over the metal flashing strip, trimmed to the width of the strip.

Bring the siding down over the flashing at the wall as cap flashing. Don't nail the siding to the flashing, and leave space between the siding and the roof to allow for painting.

Where the roof butts a masonry wall, nail the flashing to the masonry and seal the joint with a clear, non-hardening caulk. Don't nail the flashing to the roof deck.

named for the amount removed from the first shingle in each course. By removing part of the first shingle in each row, the cutouts in that course will not line up with the course below.

With the 6-inch method, also called the centered alignment method, begin the second through sixth courses with a shingle from which a multiple

Nailing tips

- Use the recommended size and grade of fasteners.

- Use four nails—one 1 inch from each end and one centered over each of the two cutouts.

- Align shingles so all nails or staples are covered by the course above.

- Drive the nails straight, not at an angle. Do not break the shingle surface with the fastener head.

- Don't drive fasteners into cracks in the roof sheathing.

- Don't nail into or above the sealing adhesive. Align each shingle correctly, and keep nails at least 2 inches from the cutouts and the end joints of the underlying course.

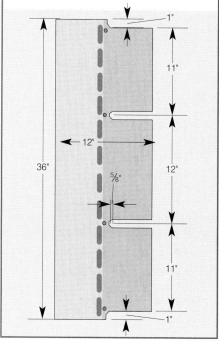

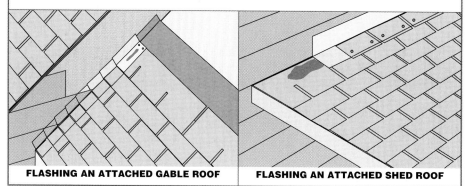

FLASHING AN ATTACHED GABLE ROOF **FLASHING AN ATTACHED SHED ROOF**

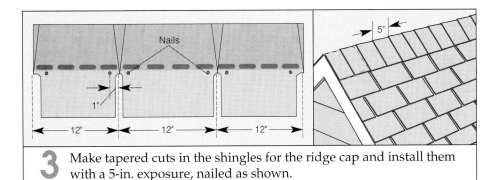

3 Make tapered cuts in the shingles for the ridge cap and install them with a 5-in. exposure, nailed as shown.

of 6 inches has been removed. It works this way: The second course starts with a shingle that has 6 inches removed; the third, with 12 inches; the fourth, with 18 inches; the fifth, with 24 inches; and the sixth, with 30 inches. The adjacent shingle in each course is full-length. Begin the seventh course with a full-length shingle, and repeat the pattern up the roof to the peak.

The 5-inch method works the same way, except that the second through seventh courses start with a shingle from which a multiple of 5 inches has been removed. The eighth course begins with a full shingle. The 4-inch method follows the same procedure, except that the trim-off is a multiple of 4 inches. Choose the method that leaves you with the widest strip at the finish end of the roof.

Some roofers use a different method than those above, starting with a shingle cut in half, a full shingle on the second course, a half shingle on the third course, and so on up the roof. To ensure a professional job, follow the manufacturer's instructions.

3 **Capping the Ridge.** Begin by cutting full shingles or pieces of scrap shingles as shown. Make sure the tapered ends are narrower than the exposed portions to end up with a neater job. Apply shingles with a 5-inch exposure. Start at the ridge end that's opposite the prevailing wind direction. Drive one nail on each side at a point about 5½ inches from the exposed end of the shingle and 1 inch up from the edge. Longer nails may be required for the cap shingles.

Closing Up Walls

To finish the sidewalls properly, you'll install all doors and windows, including trim, and finish siding to match the house.

Installing Prehung Doors

Prehung exterior doors come complete with top and side jamb pieces, stops, and in some cases thresholds. They're typically attached to the jamb assembly and held in place with shipping braces. The doors are typically 80 inches tall and come in a variety of widths from 24 to 36 inches. Most prehung doors come with complete installation instructions, including the rough opening size.

Installation Sequence. If the garage will have plywood siding attached directly to the studs, attach the siding first; then position the door jamb in the opening with the outside edge flush to the outside face of the siding. If you're installing siding over sheathing, install the door frame after you do the sheathing, but before the siding. Position the frame so it projects past the sheathing by a distance equal to the siding thickness. Then run siding up to the edges of the door jamb, and install the trim.

1 **Setting the Door in Place.** If the door comes with an attached jamb, keep the shipping braces intact. Before setting the prehung unit in place, run a couple of ¼-inch beads of non-hardening caulk between the floor and threshold for a good seal. Place the unit in the opening so that it'll swing in the desired direction. Exterior doors usually swing inward.

Remove the braces; then check the clearance between the top of the door and the head jamb: it should be a uniform ⅛ inch.

2 **Attaching the Jambs.** Use a level to plumb the hinge jamb on the face and edge, inserting shims behind the jamb at the points to be nailed. Adjust the shims to provide a uniform clearance between the jamb and the rough opening. If the jamb is twisted, insert two nails side by side through the jamb to correct the problem. Nail the jamb in three places from top to bottom.

Before attaching the lock and head jambs, recheck the tolerances. Remember, the space should be

1 Set the door in place. Check for ⅛-in. clearance at the top.

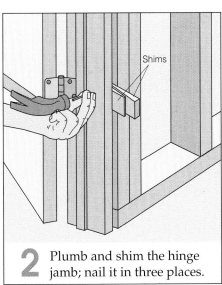

2 Plumb and shim the hinge jamb; nail it in three places.

a uniform ⅛ inch between the jamb and door. If the lock side is too tight, shim under the lock jamb to correct the situation. Plumb, shim, and nail the lock jamb to the rough opening; then shim and nail the head jamb at the center to prevent sag.

3 **Trimming the Shims.** Once you've attached all the jambs, cut off the protruding parts of the shims all around the door with a hand-saw and install the lockset, following the manufacturer's directions.

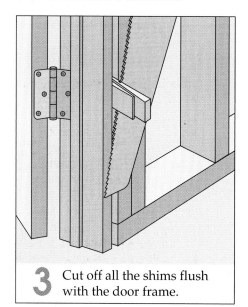

3 Cut off all the shims flush with the door frame.

Installing Windows

Decide what kind of window you want. Two common kinds of operable windows are wood-sash windows—either double-hung (shown) or casement, which open outward similarly to doors—and vinyl windows. Windows usually come with installation instructions, including the rough opening size. Whether you install the window before or after the siding depends on both the window and the siding you've chosen. Tack windows in place and test for operation before securing in position. You don't want the window to bind. Insulate the space between the window and framing members with expanding foam insulation, and seal all joints with a non-hardening caulk.

Installing Windows with Exterior Casing.
Some windows come with a casing, or brick molding, on the outside. Install the window from the outside. Center the window in the opening, and shim it. Secure the window with finishing nails through the jamb to the framing, and face-nail through the casing to the framing.

Installing Windows with Nailing Flanges.
Some windows, including aluminum windows and those made of aluminum- or vinyl-clad wood, come with a nailing flange around the outside. Nail these windows to the outside of the framing. Depending on the look you want to achieve, you can cover the flange with casing and bring the siding to the casing or cover the flange with siding, using no casing at all.

Installing a Sectional Garage Door

Before you begin the installation of the garage door, study the instructions provided by the manufacturer. Check the parts list and parts. To determine whether a part is a right-hand or left-hand one, face the door opening from the inside of the garage. Parts used on the right hand are designated RH; those used on the left are LH parts.

Where carriage bolts are installed in the track, place the bolts with the heads located on the inner side of the track to prevent interference with door movement. Bolts used as door stops are exceptions (see Step 5). When installing lag screws, drill holes with a 3/16-inch bit before driving the screws to avoid splitting the wood.

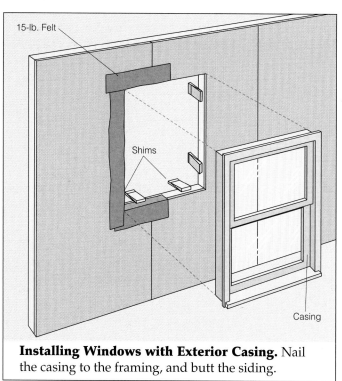

Installing Windows with Exterior Casing. Nail the casing to the framing, and butt the siding.

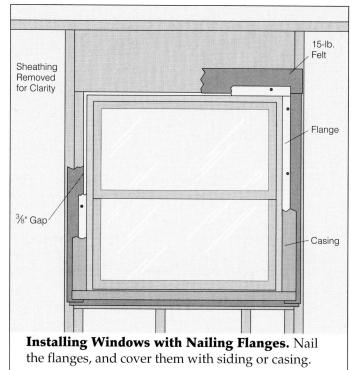

Installing Windows with Nailing Flanges. Nail the flanges, and cover them with siding or casing.

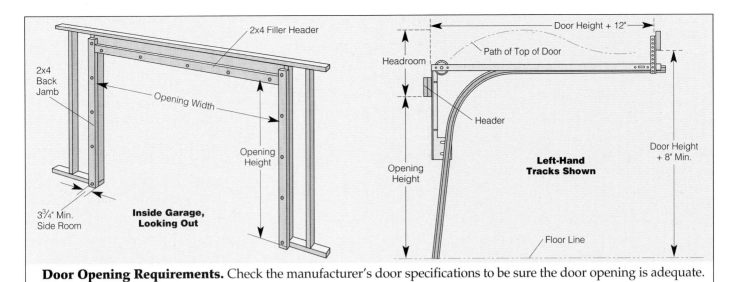

2x4 Filler Header

2x4 Back Jamb

Opening Width

Opening Height

3¾" Min. Side Room

Inside Garage, Looking Out

Door Height + 12"

Path of Top of Door

Headroom

Header

Opening Height

Left-Hand Tracks Shown

Door Height + 8" Min.

Floor Line

Door Opening Requirements. Check the manufacturer's door specifications to be sure the door opening is adequate.

Tools Required. In addition to the basic tools discussed on pages 13 to 20, you'll need a step ladder, an extension cord, locking pliers, and socket or open-end/box wrenches.

Door Opening Requirements. Check the manufacturer's literature that comes with the door to make sure your door opening provides enough operating space. Doors 6 feet 6 inches and 7 feet high, for example, are 6 feet 6 inches and 7 feet, respectively, when installed, while some so-called 8-foot-high doors actually measure 8 feet 1½ inches when installed. Make sure the door header is flush with the back jambs and that the back jambs are plumb and square. Make sure all header and jamb fasteners are flush or countersunk. Check headroom above the opening height, the back room, or the space needed for the door to open, and the horizontal track support requirements.

1 **Assembling the Vertical Tracks.** Attach the track brackets and striker plates to the vertical track members with ½-inch-long carriage bolts. The specific manufacturer instructions will tell you the correct holes to use in the vertical track.

2 **Installing the Vertical Tracks.** Position the vertical tracks so that the track brackets are against the back jambs. Locate the tops of the vertical tracks an equal distance from the top of the door. Maintain about a ¾-inch space between the edge of the door opening and the track over the full length of the vertical track to ensure proper door operation. Temporarily nail the track brackets in place with double-headed nails.

3 **Drilling Pilot Holes.** For each bracket, remove the nail and drill ³⁄₁₆-inch pilot holes into the back jambs, at the center of the slotted holes in the track brackets. Install a lag screw, and tighten it securely.

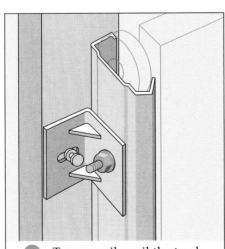

Track Bracket

Carriage Bolts

Vertical Track

Hex Washer Nut

Striker Plate

1 Attach the track brackets and striker plates to the left and right vertical tracks.

2 Temporarily nail the track brackets to the back jambs with double-headed nails.

3 Bore pilot holes in the jambs for lag screws to attach the track brackets permanently.

4 Installing the Curved Track. Assemble the curved track, flag bracket, and horizontal support angle on the floor with ½-inch-long carriage bolts and washer nuts. Line up the curved ends of the horizontal track with the vertical track, and position the track at right angles to the door opening. Vertically align the flag bracket, and nail it in place with double-headed nails. Drill ³⁄₁₆-inch pilot holes in the back jambs, through the center of the top and bottom slotted holes in the flag bracket, and install a lag screw in each pilot hole.

5 Installing the Rear Track Hangers. Determine the track hanger mounting that best suits the overhead framing as shown in A and B. Attach hangers to ceiling joists with 1½-inch lag screws. Make sure the track is level and perpendicular to the door. Measure the distance from the rear of the track to the nearest overhead joist. Cut the hanger angle to the appropriate length, and attach hanger angles to the rear of the horizontal tracks using ⁵⁄₁₆ x 1-inch-long bolts, and tighten them. Install the bolts with the heads located on the outside of the track because they'll be used to stop the top section from coming out of the track.

6 Positioning the Door. Set the door sections in place, one at a time, insert rollers (with roller brackets attached) in the track, and attach the brackets to the door sections. Secure the door sections to each other with the supplied hinges. With two or more people assisting, raise the door approximately 48 inches, and prop it open with 2x4s under the bottom brackets of the door. Make sure the bottom section is level and that about a ¾-inch spacing exists between the door and both the vertical and horizontal tracks. If the spacing is wrong, lower the door to the closed position and reposition the track hangers.

7 Installing the Operating Spring. The door operating spring may be the extension or the torsion type. We will discuss installing the extension type. Spring installation and adjustments are potentially dangerous operations, so use caution and carefully follow the instructions included in the door package.

Attach sheaves, or pulley wheels, to the horizontal support angles as shown. Pass a bolt through the sheave, washer, and round hole at the end of the horizontal angle, and secure it with a ³⁄₈-inch hex nut. Attach a sheave clevis to the spring ends, and fasten a sheave to the clevis with a bolt and nut. Place an S-hook on the opposite end of the spring, and hang it from the hanger angle. Raise the door to a

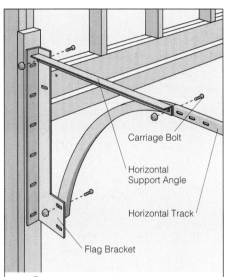

4 Assemble the curved track sections, and install them on the back jambs.

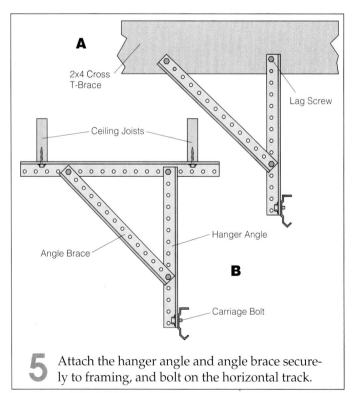

5 Attach the hanger angle and angle brace securely to framing, and bolt on the horizontal track.

6 Insert and assemble the door sections one at a time. Check for side clearance spacing.

fully open position, and prop it in place by securing locking pliers to the track under the last roller. Make sure the door is level in the opening.

8 **Threading the Lift Cable.** Attach the lift cable to the bottom corners of the door, and thread it over the front sheave, around the spring sheave, and into the end of the joiner clip. Thread the lift cable through the joiner clip as shown to prevent slippage of the lift cable. Attach the joiner clip with an S-hook in a convenient hole in the support angle. Ensure there is equal tension on both springs so that the door hangs level and in the full open position after the locking pliers are removed.

Now carefully close the door. The door should come to a gentle stop at the floor. If the door comes down hard, you will need to increase the spring tension. If the springs tend to lift the door off the floor, decrease the tension. Adjust the tension by moving the S-hook to another hole in the horizontal angle or by lengthening or shortening the cables through the joiner clips. Secure the door in an open position to adjust the spring tension.

9 **Installing the Safety Cable.** Raise the door to the full open position, and prop it in place with locking pliers. Crimp the S-hooks that hold the spring ends to the hanger angles. Thread the safety, or spring-restraint, cable through the spring, making sure the cable goes through the spring loops on each end of the spring. Loosen the nut that holds the hanger angle brace just enough to loop the cable around and retighten the nut. Attach the other end of the safety cable to the horizontal support angle with a bolt, washer, and nut.

10 **Installing the Door Stops.** With the door fully closed and latched on both sides, nail the top and side door stops to the header and jambs. Position the stops to come in contact with the door when it closes but not to interfere with its operation.

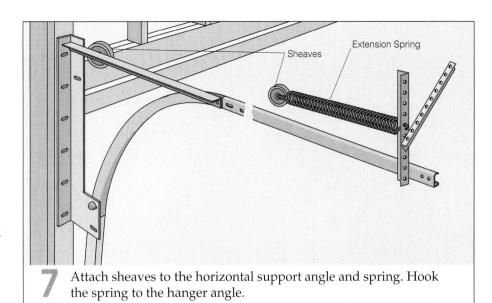

7 Attach sheaves to the horizontal support angle and spring. Hook the spring to the hanger angle.

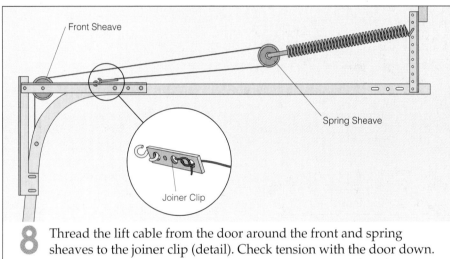

8 Thread the lift cable from the door around the front and spring sheaves to the joiner clip (detail). Check tension with the door down.

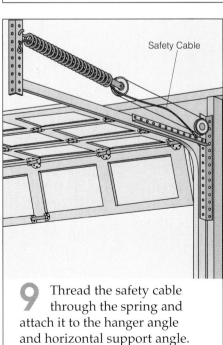

9 Thread the safety cable through the spring and attach it to the hanger angle and horizontal support angle.

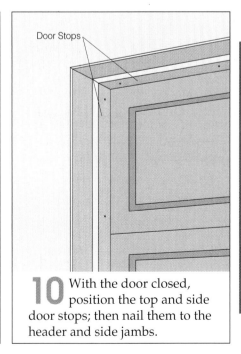

10 With the door closed, position the top and side door stops; then nail them to the header and side jambs.

Connecting to the Existing House

Make the garage or carport accessible from the house through a door connecting the two. If you're adding at the kitchen area of the house, you can usually locate the attached unit to take advantage of the existing door. If an existing door is not available, the next best solution is enlarging an existing window opening to accommodate a doorway. Converting a window to a door results in less loss of usable floor space.

If you must make a doorway in an existing wall to connect the garage or carport to the house, try to avoid having to reroute wiring and plumbing lines. Use care in removing the interior and exterior wall finish. Take off only that portion necessary to frame the door opening.

Siding

Siding material is commonly available in plywood, solid wood, aluminum, and vinyl. Common wood siding types include shingles or shakes and clapboard and other board types. Aluminum and vinyl siding in the board style is installed horizontally.

Installing Horizontal Wood Siding

Wood siding may have rabbeted joints, tongue-and-groove joints, or overlapping joints, as with beveled clapboard siding. Eastern white pine, western white pine, red cedar, white cedar, sugar pine, redwood, cypress, Douglas fir, southern yellow pine, and ponderosa pine make quality board siding. Use 6d galvanized ring- or spiral-shanked nails. Wrap corners and window and door openings with 15-lb. roofing felt to protect against moisture intrusion.

1 Installing the Starter Strip. The starter strip isn't necessary for siding that has rabbeted or tongue-and-groove joints. Make the strip out of stock that's 2 or 3 inches wide and as thick as the siding at the point of

the course overlap. Nail the strip along the base of the wall just above the foundation.

2 Getting a Level Start. Don't assume the foundation is level. Mark the height of the top of the first siding course at both corners of the wall. Snap a chalk line and check it with a spirit level. If the line isn't level, hold a piece of siding against the wall with one end at the low point of the chalk line. Place the level on top of the board and mark the opposite end when it's level. Mark a new guideline.

3 Cutting the Siding. Use a circular saw or power miter saw to get quick square cuts. Use a finish crosscut blade. Cut and attach all

pieces so they end at a wall stud for firm nailing.

4 Marking the Next Course. After installing each piece of siding, mark it with a guideline for the bottom of the next course. Make the marks with a chalk line or a pencil and combination square.

5 Nailing the Siding. For the next course, tack a nail at the course guideline where one end of the siding will be nailed. Rest the end of the siding on this nail. At the opposite end of the board, begin nailing at the second stud from the end. Position the nails just above the overlap for beveled siding and just above the rabbet for rabbeted siding.

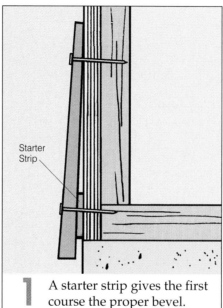

Starter Strip

1 A starter strip gives the first course the proper bevel.

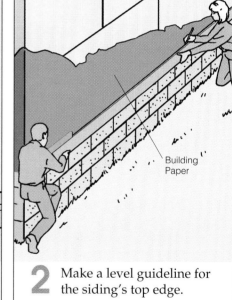

Building Paper

2 Make a level guideline for the siding's top edge.

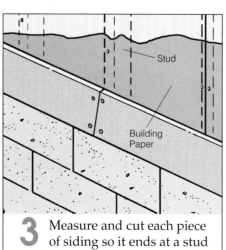

Stud

Building Paper

3 Measure and cut each piece of siding so it ends at a stud for solid nailing at the joint.

Course Line

4 Mark succeeding course lines with a square or chalk line.

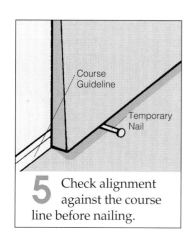

5 Check alignment against the course line before nailing.

6 To avoid splitting the wood at the ends, drill pilot holes for nails.

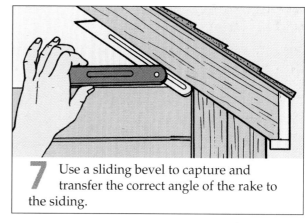

7 Use a sliding bevel to capture and transfer the correct angle of the rake to the siding.

Blind-nail tongue-and-groove siding at an angle through the tongue. Double-check the alignment of the course before hammering the nail home. Check the opposite end, and nail it at least one stud in from the end. Remove the tack and complete the nailing.

6 Nailing the Joints. When you add adjacent pieces, nail the joints last. Be sure to drill pilot holes to avoid splitting the wood. Add three or four additional courses, being careful to stagger joints. At every fourth or fifth course, check the siding board with a spirit level and make adjustments accordingly.

7 Capturing the Gable Angle. Use a sliding bevel to capture the angle of the rake for transfer to the piece of siding to be cut. Align the body of the tool with the top edge of an installed board and adjust the blade to run along the slope of the rake. As an alternative, make a template of the angle using scrap held against the underside of the rake.

8 Locating the Angle. Locate the angle on the board by measuring along the course guideline, and cut the board accordingly. Save the scrap as a marking guide for other pieces.

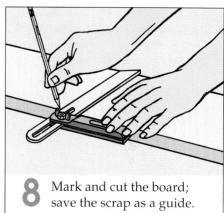

8 Mark and cut the board; save the scrap as a guide.

To avoid splits, especially in small pieces, drill pilot holes for nails nearest the rake. Caulk the joint between the siding and trim.

Corner Treatments

Corners have an impact on the appearance of a building and affect the difficulty of the job.

Mitered Corners. Creating mitered corners requires skill and a circular saw, power miter saw, or radial-arm saw. Galvanized 6d nails join the two edges of the siding. Drill pilot holes before nailing.

Metal Corners. Corner cap made from metal allow for error and are an easy and neat finish. Don't wrap them too tightly around the corner.

Outside Corner Boards. If you want to use outside corner boards, install them before you install the siding. Cut the siding to meet the trim squarely with a butt joint.

Attach the boards with 8d galvanized common nails about every 16 inches.

Inside Corner Boards. As with outside corners, install these boards with galvanized 8d nails before siding. Butt the siding against it on both sides.

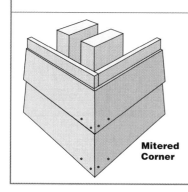

Mitered Corner

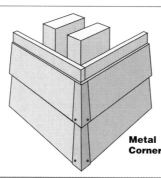

Metal Corner

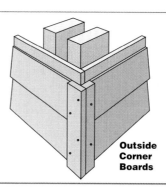

Outside Corner Boards

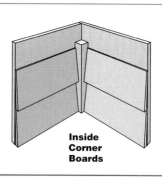

Inside Corner Boards

Installing Wood Shingles and Shakes

Shingles are thinner than shakes and are sawn smooth on both sides. Shakes often are split by hand rather than cut and have an irregular shape. Shakes are thicker and more durable than shingles. Match what you have on your house. You'll use two grades of shingles or shakes: undercourse (No. 3) and finish (No. 1).

The maximum weather exposure manufacturers recommend for No. 1 grade shingles varies depending on their size: 12 inches for 16-inch shingles, 14 inches for 18-inch shingles, and 16 inches for 24-inch shingles. Shakes that are 18 inches long may be installed at exposures up to 14 inches; 24-inch shakes, up to 18 inches. Of course, you can use smaller exposures, down to 4 or 5 inches.

1 Installing the Starter Course. Measure to make sure there will be at least a 4-inch course of shingles beneath the eaves. The first course must overlap the sheathing by about 1 inch. Snap a chalk line on the foundation wall as a guideline. Install a two-layer row of No. 3 undercourse shingles (subsequent courses to get one-layer rows), leaving ⅛ to ¼ inch between each shingle to allow for expansion. Use galvanized roofing nails 1 inch above the butt line. Then install a layer of finish shingles, extending them at least ½ inch below the butt line of the first two layers. Overlap all joints between shingles.

2 Nailing the Double Course. Use 6d galvanized ring-shank nails to nail the finish shingles 2 inches above the butt line and ¾ inch from both edges. Nail un-dercourse shingles with one nail about 2 inches from the top edge. The face course nails penetrate these shingles to hold them in place.

3 Adding Courses. Use a 1x4 tacked along the butt line as a guide to shingle installation. Undercourse shingles rest on the tops of the face shingles of the previous course. When you need to trim shingles, cut them with a roofing hatchet, utility knife, or table saw. Smooth the edge with a block plane if needed.

4 Finishing at the Eaves. Nail the eave pieces (remember, at least 4 inches long) near the top with galvanized finishing nails.

5 Capturing the Gable-End Angle. The sliding bevel is the best tool for cutting shingles and shakes to the correct angle under the gable ends. Use the bevel to capture the angle and mark the correct cut line. Use the first whole shingle in the course as a plumb edge for setting the bevel. Cut a shingle, and trim it. Keep the shingle cutoff as a template for cutting others.

Installing Vinyl/Aluminum Siding

Aluminum siding is available in many board profiles, as is vinyl siding, and comes with essentially the same accessories required for installation. The two sidings are installed in much the same way.

1 The starter course gets two layers. Install the face layer ½ in. below the butt edge.

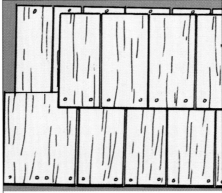

2 Nail the face shingles 2 in. above the butt line and at least ¾ in. from each edge.

3 Tack the guide board; rest the undercourse shingles on the previous face shingles.

4 Fasten partial shingles under the eaves using galvanized finishing nails.

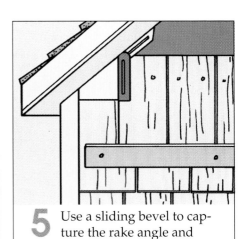

5 Use a sliding bevel to capture the rake angle and transfer it to the shingles.

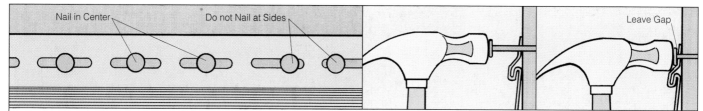

Installing Aluminum/Vinyl Siding. Nail in the center of the nailing slots (left) and just far enough to leave a slight gap between the nailhead and the siding (right). Drive the nails at a 90-deg. angle so there's minimal friction as the panel slides (middle).

Vinyl siding is loose fitting and does not provide resistance to air infiltration. Seal air-leakage paths before installing the siding. Aviation snips readily cut vinyl panels and accessories. Square a line across the panel and cut the top interlock first, cutting toward the bottom of the panel. Panels may also be cut with a power saw or handsaw. Reversing the blade on the power saw gives the best results and is a must in cold weather to prevent splitting and chipping the panel. To make lengthwise cuts, use a straightedge and utility knife. Score the panel, and bend it until it breaks.

Vinyl siding expands and contracts with temperature changes and must be installed in a manner to permit movement on the nail shank. Don't drive nails all the way so as to bind the panel. Locate the nails near the center of the nailing slot so the siding can move, and drive the nails straight. Cut the panels ¼ inch short between two solid objects, such as two windows or a window and corner post, to allow a ⅛-inch gap for expansion at each end. Lap panels 1½ inches to allow ½ inch for movement.

Use corrosion-resistant nails with a ⅛-inch-diameter shank and a 5⁄16-inch head 1½ to 1¾ inches long. For walls having insulating sheathing, use nails long enough to penetrate the framing ¾ inch. If you're afraid of hitting siding when nailing in close proximity, use a nail set to drive the nail home.

1 Installing Trim. Attach the outside corner trim, hanging it from the top by a nail. Add any inside corner posts; then add J-trim around windows and doors and along the gable ends.

2 Installing the Starter Strip. Start the siding by snapping a chalk line for the starter strip around the structure parallel to the sill plate. Align the starter strip with this line and nail it in place on 8-inch centers through the nailing slots. Leave ¼ inch between the corner-post nailing flange and the end of the starter strip.

3 Installing the Panels. Start installation at the back of the structure and work toward the front, overlapping the panels away from the entrance ways. Install the first panel in the interlock of the starter strip, and make sure it's locked. Secure the panel by nailing through the nailing slots 12 to 16 inches apart. Continue

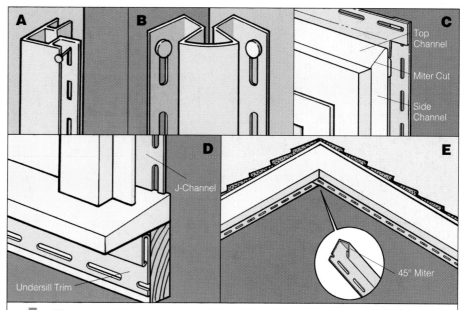

1 Hang outside corner posts (A); add inside corner posts (B); lap top over side J-channel around widows and doors (C); attach any undersill trim to wood furring (D); install J-channel along the gable ends (E).

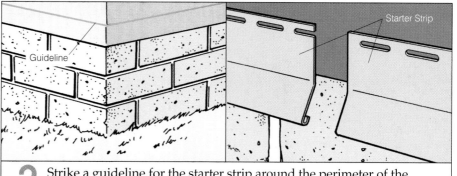

2 Strike a guideline for the starter strip around the perimeter of the structure (left), and nail the strip in place (right).

6 Finishing Up

installation in this manner, avoiding vertical alignment of the joints. To ensure neat end laps, don't nail closer than 10 inches to the end of the overlapping panel, and notch the nailing flange.

4 **Fitting at Eaves and Window Openings.** After measuring and cutting off the siding nailing flange at the desired location, use a snap lock punch to provide lugs that grab the undersill trim nailed under the window or the eaves to hold the upper part of the panel in place.

5 **Soffit Applications.** Install F soffit channels at the wall and at the edge of the fascia, securing them through the nailing slots about 10 inches on center. Cut alternate perforated and non-perforated soffit

panels ⅛ inch shorter than the inside dimensions from one soffit channel to the opposite one. Where a soffit

turns a corner (see drawing), install two J-channels back to back to form an H-member.

Special Tools

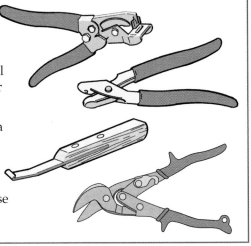

Nail Slot Punch. When you have to nail and there is no slot, the nail slot punch makes one.

Snap Lock Punch. Makes a small lug that engages in the trim under windowsills and eaves.

Zip Tool. Hooks under the lip of a joint as you pull the tool along to release or lock the siding in place.

Aviation Snips. For a clean, smooth cut, do not completely close the blades at the end of a cut.

3 Lock the first-course siding panel into the starter strip (left). Continue to interlock panels (middle), and form laps away from entrances by notching the nailing flange (right).

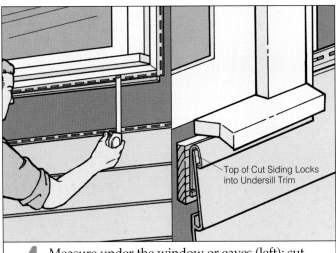

4 Measure under the window or eaves (left); cut the panel to size; use the snap lock lugs; and snap the panel into the undersill trim (right).

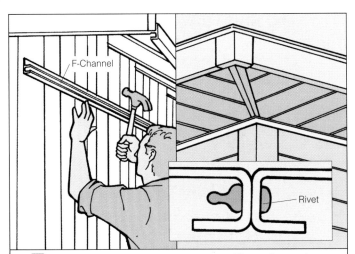

5 Snap a guideline and install soffit F-channel on the wall and on the inside edge of the fascia. Rivet pieces of J-channel for a mitered joint.

garage projects

One-Car Detached Garage with Gable Roof

This one-car detached garage is a simple structure that will satisfy simple demands. The minimum dimensions for a one-car unit are 10 feet in width and 20 feet in length, measured from the face of the inside studs. Keep in mind that these dimensions are minimum standards. You should never make the garage smaller, but you can feel free to increase the dimensions to make the garage both wider and longer to accommodate storage, washer-and-dryer space, a work bench, and the like.

The interior dimensions of this garage are slightly larger than minimum requirements, to allow a little extra room for a swinging side door and for some storage or shelving on the rear wall. In

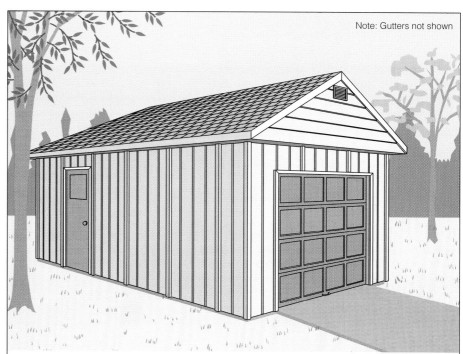

Note: Gutters not shown

One-Car Detached Garage with Gable Roof. A simple structure with a simple purpose, this garage provides space for a car plus a small amount of storage.

Cutting & Materials List

NAME	QTY	SIZE
Foundation[1]		
Ready-mix concrete for concrete footing (12" wide x 6" thick)	1½ cu. yd.	
Hollow-core concrete block for foundation wall, if required, per perimeter course	49	8" x 8" x 16"
Masonry cement (for 100 blocks)	1	70-lb. bag
Sand (for 100 blocks)	3 cu. ft.	
Gravel for 4" floor base	3¼ cu. yd.	
Sand for 1" min. cap on gravel	1¾ cu. yd.	
Polyethylene vapor barrier (6-mil)	270 sq. ft.	
Ready-mix concrete for 4-inch-thick floor slab	3½ cu. yd.	
Anchor bolts	14	½" dia.
Framing		
Sill plate (pressure treated)	2	22' 2x4s
	1	12' 2x4
	2	24" 2x4s
Sill plate gasket	57 lin. ft.	
Bottom plate	2	22' 2x4s
	1	12' 2x4
	2	24" 2x4s

NAME	QTY	SIZE
Studs (16" o.c.)		
Corner posts	12	8' 2x4s
Spacer blocks	12	12" 2x4s
King studs	8	8' 2x4s
Jamb studs	8	84" 2x4s
Regular studs	33	8' 2x4s
Cripple studs	2	8' 2x4s (cut to fit)
Gable-end studs	4	12' 2x4s (cut to fit)
Top plate and cap	4	22' 2x4s
	4	12' 2x4s
Headers		
Windows	4	40" 2x12s
Door	2	41" 2x12s
	2	10' 2x12s
Window sills	2	48" 2x4s
Ceiling joists (16" o.c.)	18	12' 2x6s
Rafters (16" o.c.)	40	9' 2x6s
Ridgeboard	1	16' 2x8
	1	10' 2x8
Sway braces (uprights)	2	48" 2x4s
Sway braces (horizontals)	2	60" 2x4s
Sub-fascia (eaves)	2	16' 2x8s
	2	10' 2x8s
Wall sheathing	16	½" x 4' x 9' plywood or OSB
Roof sheathing	15	½" x 4' x 8' plywood

addition to the side access door, there are windows on the rear and right-side walls to allow light and ventilation. The gable roof, with an 8-in-12 slope, is good for any climate and has a generous overhang of 16 inches. As designed, the garage has grooved plywood siding on the four walls with wood clapboard siding on the gable ends. You can use any siding you want.

Starting the Garage

All the project plans in this chapter assume a 6-inch-thick footing, which must go below the frost line in your area, with an integrated slab. Depending on your circumstances, you may need to build a foundation stem wall to bridge the footing and slab. If you use the stem wall as a foundation for the stud walls, the sill plate will have to be the same thickness as the foundation wall.

The materials lists assume you'll use the slab as the foundation, and so specify 2x4 mudsills. If you build on a foundation stem wall made of the 8-inch concrete block shown in the lists, you'll need 2x8 mudsills.

The cutting and materials lists for this project and the others show the lumber sizes you'll need for each element of the project, but often you can cut a number of these pieces from one longer length. The mudsills

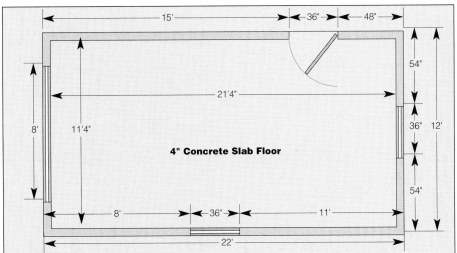

Starting the Garage. This floorplan shows the footprint of the garage, with a side access door, two windows, and room at the rear for shelving.

Name	Qty	Size
Roofing, Siding, and Finish		
15-lb. Roofing felt (single layer)	520 sq. ft.	
Metal drip edge	90 lin. ft.	
Three-tab composite shingles	500 sq. ft.	
Plywood panel siding	16	⅜" x 4' x 9' panels
Gable-end clapboard siding	132 sq. ft.	
Corner boards	4	9' 1x4s
	4	9' 1x3s
Battens	13	9' 1x2s
Soffits	4	⅜" x 4 'x 8' panels (cut 16"wide)
Soffit crown molding	80 lin. ft.	
Attic vents	2	18" x 12"
Soffit vents	4	8" x 12"
Exterior entrance door	1	36" x 80" (prehung)
Door lockset	1	
Double-hung windows	2	36" x 48"
Sash locks	2	
Sectional garage door	1	8' x 78" door
Top garage-door stop	1	8' 1x4

Name	Qty	Size
Garage door facing	1	10' 1x4
	2	8' 1x4s
Gutter system		
Gutter	50 lin. ft.	
Drop outlets	4	
Elbows	12	
Downspouts	4	10' sections
Right end caps	2	
Left end caps	2	
Gutter connectors	4	
Gutter brackets	20	
Downspout brackets	12	
Nails for installing:		
Wall framing (tilt-up)	12 lbs.	16d
Ceiling joists to top plate	1¼ lbs.	8d
Rafters & bracing	1¼ lbs.	8d
	4½ lbs.	16d
Gable-end studs	1¼ lbs.	8d
Wall sheathing	9½ lbs.	8d
Roof sheathing	5½ lbs.	8d
Roofing felt and drip edge	¾ lbs.	2d roofing nails
Shingles	6½ lbs.	3d roofing nails
Siding	3 lbs.	8d alum.
Soffit	1 lb.	4d finish
Molding (facing & trim)	2 lbs.	6d finish
"H" clips for roof sheathing panels (if required)		
Paint and caulk		

¹ Size and quantity of forming lumber for concrete footings and slab depend on the footing depth and forming method.

for the rear and front walls, for example, are shown as a 12-foot 2x4 and 2 24-inch 2x4s, respectively, but you can cut the sills from a single 16-foot 2x4. The same is true for the bottom plate, as well as a number of other framing elements. As another example, the 8 84-inch jamb studs can be cut from 4 14-foot 2x4s.

Framing the Garage

Once you've laid out the garage and poured the foundation, you'll start framing the structure, following the procedures on pages 39 to 50. As you can see from the accompanying drawings, the garage is a straight-forward building, with lots of straight, uncomplicated lines—a good project to hone your construction skills.

Set the sill gasket and sill plates over the anchor bolts. Lay out the studs on the top and bottom plates, being sure to account for all window and door openings with headers and king and jack studs. You can lay the sill and bottom plates across small openings like utility doors and cut them out later.

The cutting and materials list shows 8-foot 2x4s for all studs, but you can use shorter pieces, called precuts, if your lumber supplier or home center sells them. Precuts come in sizes down to about 7½ feet; you can use them because you're building 8-foot high walls and the mudsill, bottom plate, top plate, and cap plate make up 6 inches.

Once you've erected the shell of the structure and nailed together all the stud walls at the corners, you can start building the roof. (See pages 46 to 50.) Install the ceiling joists, then measure and cut the rafters for an 8-in-12 slope. Lay out rafter placement on the top plates and ridgeboard, then raise the roof. With the structure framed out, the next step is to sheathe it and install the roofing to close it in. You can sheathe the walls with plywood siding alone or use plywood or OSB sheathing and plywood siding, as given in the cutting and materials list.

Finishing the Garage

Once the building is closed up, you can install the windows and doors. The garage door is perhaps the most difficult to install, but even that isn't as hard as it may seem, as you can see on pages 56 to 59. Grooved plywood panels, also called T1-11 plywood, form the siding on the four walls. The gable-end walls get a different treatment, with wood clapboards. You cut the rake angle for the siding using a scrap piece of wood to scribe the angle in place or by using an adjustable sliding bevel. (See page 61.) Of course, you can use any siding you wish—to match or complement your house, for example—but if you use wood and/or wood panels, you'll have to paint or stain the siding to your tastes.

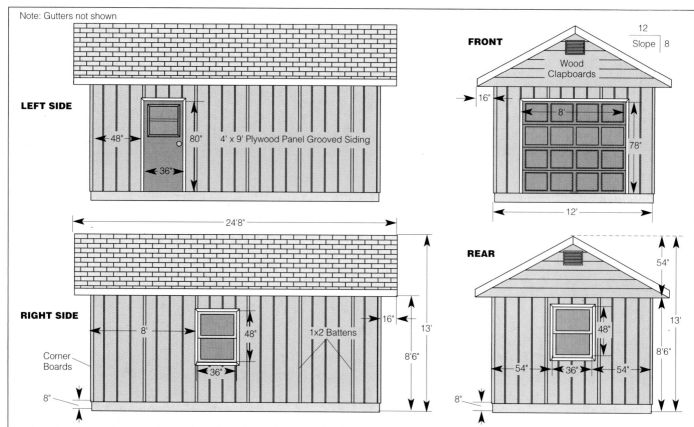

Framing the Garage. Elevation drawings showing both sides of the garage (left) give size and placement of the side window and access door. The front and rear elevations (right) show important dimensions, as well as how the garage will look from the street.

One-Car Attached Carport with Shed Roof

A carport is simply an attached or detached garage without walls, or parts of walls, and a garage door. The carport shown here has a brick skirt wall on its long side and an enclosed rear portion that's essen-tially a 5 x 11-foot storage shed. The construction sequence and most of the construction techniques are the same as if you were to build a garage. (See pages 66 to 68.) The main difference is the location and construction of the support posts and headers, which serve the same function as load-bearing walls in a garage. The carport shown here uses steel columns with a 0.237-inch wall thickness and top and bottom plates with two ½-inch-diameter holes in each plate for anchor bolts. You'll use four ³⁄₁₆ x 2½-inch lag screws to mount the top post plate to the header and four ³⁄₁₆ x 4-inch bolts with washers and end nuts to mount the bottom post plate to the masonry skirt wall. As with a garage, the minimum dimension for the carport should be 10 x 20 feet. The carport shown here is somewhat larger.

Adding onto a House

Decide how you'll join the roof to the house during the planning stage. Try to use a method of joining that results in the least amount of changes to the house. The less you tear off, the less the expense and labor of putting it back together.

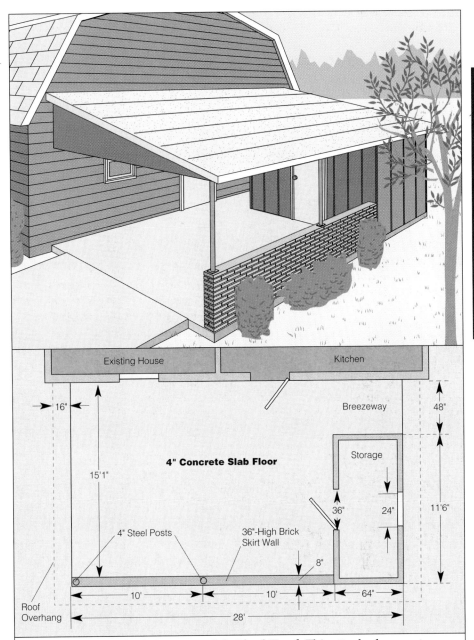

One-Car Attached Carport with Shed Roof. This attached carport features basic protection with a plus—an enclosed storage area at the rear.

Cutting & Materials List

NAME	QTY	SIZE
Foundation[1]		
Ready-mix concrete for footing (12" wide x 6" thick)	1½ cu. yd.	
Hollow-core concrete block for foundation wall, if required, per perimeter course	42	8" x 8" x 16"
Masonry cement (for 100 blocks)	1	70-lb. bag
Sand (for 100 blocks)	3 cu. ft.	

NAME	QTY	SIZE
Anchor bolts	10	½" dia
Rebar for skirt wall	5	½" x 12" (4" in slab, 8" in brickwork)
Gravel for 4" floor base	4¾ cu. yd.	
Sand for 1" min. cap on gravel	2½ cu. yd.	
Polyethylene vapor barrier (6-mil)	425 sq. ft.	
Ready-mix concrete for 4-inch-thick floor slab	5 cu. yd.	

Name	Qty	Size
Steel columns	2	4" dia. x 5' long
Brick	800	Standard brick
Mortar (for ⅜" mortar joint)	7.87 cu. ft.	
Flexible metal wall ties	30	
Framing		
Sill plate gasket	32 lin. ft.	
Sill plate (pressure treated)	3	12' 2x4s
Bottom plate	3	12' 2x4s
Studs (16" o.c.)		
Corner posts	12	8' 2x4s
Spacer blocks	12	12" 2x4s
King studs	4	8' 2x4s
Jamb studs	4	84" 2x4s
Wall studs	18	8' 2x4s
Cripple studs	1	10' 2x4 (cut to fit)
Top plate and cap	6	12' 2x4s
Headers		
Window	2	28" 2x12s
Door	2	41" 2x12s
Open-Span Header	2	20' 2x8s
Window sill	1	26" 2x4
Ceiling joists/rafters (16" o.c.)	22	18' 2x8s
Sub-fascia (eaves)	2	14' 2x8s
Fascia boards	7	10' 1x10s
Cripples at roof ends joining the plates to the ceiling joists	2	14' 2x4s (cut to fit)
Ledger	2	14' 2x6s
Wall sheathing (optional)	9	½" x 4' x 8' plywood
Roof sheathing	18	½" x 4' x 8' plywood
Roofing, Siding, and Finish		
15-lb. Roofing felt	500 sq. ft.	
Metal drip edge	62 lin. ft.	
Roll roofing	5	90-lb. rolls

Name	Qty	Size
Plastic roofing cement	3 gal.	
10" Wide metal flashing	30 lin. ft.	
Grooved panel siding	9	⅜" x 4' x 9' panels
Corner boards	4	9' 1x3s
	4	9' 1x2s
Shed roof ends	2	⅜" x 4' x 8' plywood
Horizontal batten	1	16' 1x4
Soffits (exterior plywood)	3	⅜" x 4' x 8'(cut to fit)
Eave ventilator	28 lin. ft.	
Exterior door	1	36" x 80" prehung
Door lockset	1	
Double-hung window	1	24" x 30"
Sash lock	1	
Gutter system		
Gutter	28 lin. ft.	
Drop outlets	2	
Elbows	6	
Downspouts	2	10' sections
Right end cap	1	
Left end cap	1	
Gutter connectors	3	
Gutter brackets	10	
Downspout brackets	6	
Nails for installing		
Wall framing	8 lbs.	16d
Ceiling joists to ledger & header	3.5 lbs.	16d
Header beam assembly	½ lb.	16d
Shed-end cripples	½ lb.	8d
Wall sheathing	5 lbs.	8d
Roofing felt and drip edge	¾ lb.	2d roofing nails
Roll roofing	3¾ lbs.	2d roofing nails
Exterior wall panel siding	1 lb.	8d alum. casing head
Soffit, ceiling, facing & trim molding	1 lb.	6d finishing
Paint and caulk		

¹ Size and quantity of forming lumber for concrete footings and slab depend on the footing depth and forming method.

Structural Considerations. You'll most likely tie the carport roof to the wall of the house in a manner that supports the weight of the roof so that the house becomes the bearing wall for much of the roof weight. Wall studs spaced 16 or 24 inches on center are able to absorb the additional weight. You can also furnish structural support for the carport roof by butting posts to the house wall. Regardless of the support you use, make sure the system is structurally sound and rigid enough to support the roof dead load plus live loads of ice, snow, and wind. Also, the tie-in must meet the requirements of your local code.

Tearing Off Siding. If it's necessary to remove house siding, clear away only that portion necessary to join the roof. Take off each piece carefully because you may need to reinstall part of the siding after the carport roof is built. You can remove most siding types without damage using the proper tools. Pull nails with a pry bar, cat's paw, or claw hammer. Use a vinyl siding zip tool to disconnect the panel lock joints.

Temporary Weather Protection. Whenever you remove a portion of the exterior finish wall, the underlying wall sheathing, if any, exposed framing members, insulation, and back

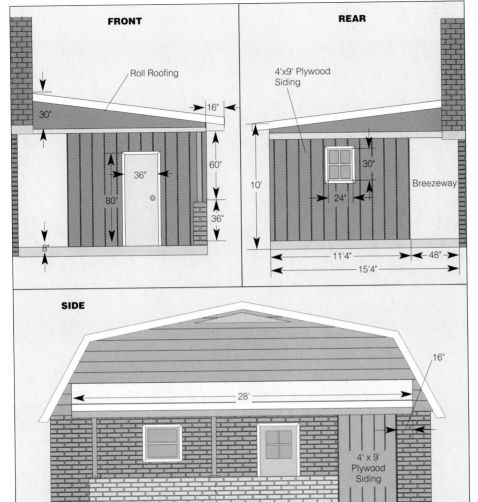

Adding onto a House. In most cases, you'll use a ledger to bear the weight of the new roof when you add a shed-roof carport to an existing house. Make the roof a minimum 2-in-12 slope.

side of the interior finish wall material are exposed to the weather. Certain types of wall sheathing, such as plywood, OSB, fiberboard, and plastic insulating board, are not harmed by a short duration of exposure. You should, however, weather-protect all openings with roofing felt, polyethylene, or other suitable covering. Openings in the roof or gable end can expose the ceiling area to serious water damage if not covered.

Fire Walls/Ceilings/Doors. A carport entirely open on two or more sides need not have a fire separation wall between the carport and the house. (See page 12.) An enclosed carport

requires a fire wall between the carport and the house, must have a fire resistant ceiling, and requires that any window between the carport and house be fixed.

The door entering the carport from the house can be any type. Any sash in the door must be the fixed type (non-operable), and the door must be self-closing. These restrictions prevent exhaust fumes from entering the dwelling. A car idling in the carport with a breeze blowing through an open window or door can be harmful or fatal to the inhabitants sleeping inside.

Attaching Ledgers

Ledgers attached to the house framing or a brick exterior wall can support the roof framing and tie the carport to the house. Give the roof adequate slope to ensure proper water runoff. The plan shown here uses a 2-in-12 roof slope.

Install on the house a 2x6 treated ledger the length of the carport framing that joins the house. Attach the ledger to wall studs or other structural members like the top plate with two 20d nails at each stud and 16 inches on center at the top plate. You may use ³⁄₁₆ x 3½-inch lag screws with washers in lieu of nails.

Secure the ledger to a brick wall using ³⁄₁₆ x 3½-inch lag screws secured to expansion sleeves inserted in the brick. Drill a hole in the brick (not a mortar joint) the diameter required to receive the expansion sleeve. Insert the sleeve flush with the face of the brick. Fit the lag screw through a pre-drilled hole in the ledger and tighten it. Use a washer on the lag screw; don't overtighten it. Make sure the sleeve is positioned in the solid portion of the brick. Install lag screws 16 inches on center.

Exterior Trim for Posts and Headers

To ensure the structural integrity of wood posts and headers, use pressure-treated lumber or protect the members from the weather. For the proper finish look, cover the posts and headers with finish materials.

Materials. Finish-grade exterior plywood and wood boards are common materials used to cover and protect posts and headers while offering a finished appearance. Use trim pieces like outside corner moldings to cover the raw corner edges. Other moldings in the crown, cove, seam, and cap patterns are available to "kill" raw joints of all types—wherever they might occur. Molding is available in paint or stain grade.

Installation Techniques. Cut exterior material, such as 8-foot panels, lengthwise and the width of posts and the height of headers. Install the panels with 6d finishing nails spaced 16 inches apart along both edges of the post and the height of header members. Apply trim pieces with 6d finishing nails spaced 12 inches apart.

Thicker material like boards can be mitered at butt and edge joints for a neat finished appearance, eliminating the need for molding. Countersink nails and fill the nailholes with putty after applying a prime coat. When staining, use a color-matching putty.

Slanted Walls. A side wall in an open carport running along the slope of the shed roof is a slanted wall in that each stud is a different length. The top plate thus is sloped and runs parallel with the slope of the roof.

Install the top plate of the wall from corner post to corner post and mark the bottom plate for the selected stud spacing. Using a stud member slightly longer than the height of the wall, position it on the stud layout mark at one end of the bottom plate. Plumb the stud with a level, and scribe the top of the stud at the bottom edge of the top plate, indicating the length of the stud and the angle of the cut. Plumb and mark the remaining studs in like manner, and toenail them to the top and bottom plates with 8d nails.

Two-Car Detached Garage with Truss Roof

The minimum dimensions for a two-car unit are 18 feet 4 inches in width and 20 feet in length. The garage shown here is 20 x 28 feet, providing ample space for storage and vehicles. Plan your unit dimensions in 24-inch increments when possible to make the best use of standard length and width building materials.

To make the job go easier, plan on building your two-car garage with roof trusses. Trusses are ideal for long spans since they're engineered to span the dimension from sidewall to sidewall without intermediate sup-

Cutting & Materials List

Name	Qty	Size
Foundation[1]		
Ready-mix concrete for footing (12" wide x 6" thick)	2 cu. yd.	
Hollow-core concrete block for foundation wall, if required, per perimeter course	70	8" x 8" x 16"
Masonry cement (for 100 blocks)	1	70-lb. bag
Sand (for 100 blocks)	3 cu. ft.	
Gravel for 4" floor base	7 cu. yd.	
Sand for 1" min. cap on gravel	3½ cu. yd.	
Polyethylene vapor barrier (6-mil)	560 sq. ft.	
Ready-mix concrete for 4-inch-thick floor slab	5¼ cu. yd.	
Anchor bolts	18	½" dia.
Framing		
Sill plate gasket	92 lin. ft.	
Sill plate (pressure-treated)	4	14' 2x4s
	1	20' 2x4
	2	24" 2x4s
Bottom plate	4	14' 2x4s
	1	20' 2x4
	2	24" 2x4s
Studs (16" o.c.)		
Corner posts	12	8' 2x4s
Spacer blocks	12	12" 2x4s
King studs	14	8' 2x4s
Jamb studs	14	84" 2x4s

Name	Qty	Size
Wall studs	59	8' 2x4s
Cripple studs	3	12' 2x4s (cut to fit)
Top plate	4	14' 2x4s
	2	20' 2x4s
Top plate caps	2	16' 2x4s
	2	12' 2x4s
	2	20' 2x4s
Headers		
Windows	6	35" 2x12s
36" Door	2	41" 2x12s
78" Closet door	2	83" 2x6s
32" Door	2	37" 2x6s
Garage door	2	18' 2x12s
Window sill	3	31" 2x4s
Roof trusses (24" o.c.) 6-in-12 slope	13	22' 8" wide
Gable-end trusses with studs 16" o.c.	2	
Truss spacer blocks at eaves	4	14' 2x4s (cut to fit)
Ridgeboard spacer blocks	2	14' 2x4s (cut to fit)
Temporary braces for installing trusses	8	8' 1x4s
	4	16' 1x4s
Sway braces	2	8' 2x4s
Sub-fascia (eaves)	4	16' 2x6s
Wall sheathing	20	½" x 4' x 8' plywood
Roof sheathing	28	½" x 4' x 8' plywood

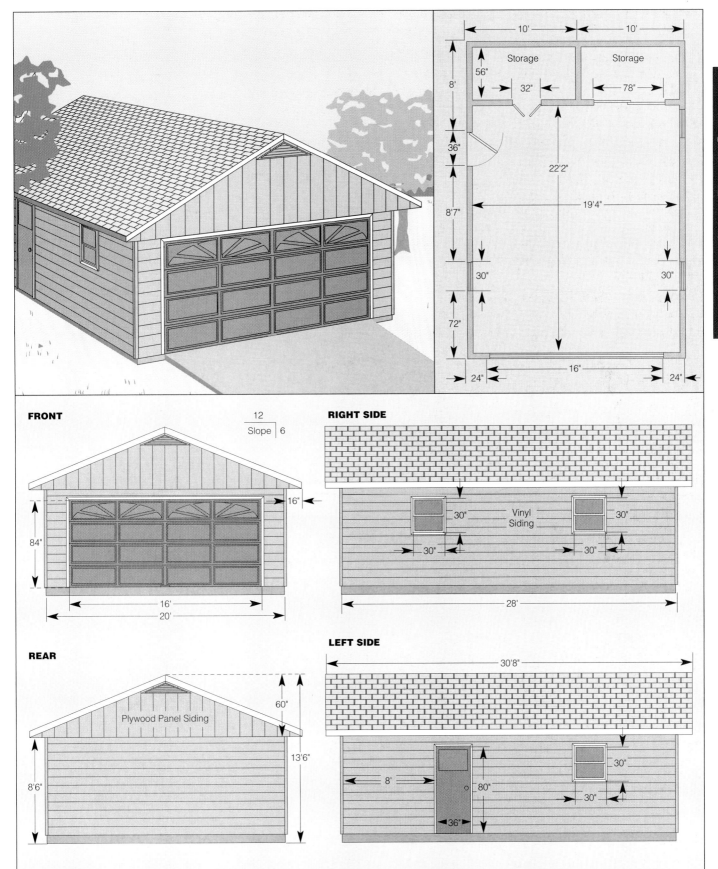

FRONT

Slope $\frac{12}{6}$

16"
84"
16'
20'

RIGHT SIDE

Vinyl Siding
30"
30"
30"
30"
28'

LEFT SIDE

30'8"
8'
80"
36"
30"
30"

REAR

Plywood Panel Siding
60"
13'6"
8'6"

Floor plan:
10'
10'
Storage
Storage
56"
8'
32"
78"
36"
22'2"
8'7"
19'4"
30"
30"
72"
24"
16"
24"

Two-Car Detached Garage with Truss Roof. Besides offering shelter for two cars, a well designed garage will provide ample space for other kinds of storage as well.

Name	Qty	Size	Name	Qty	Size
Roofing, Siding, and Finish			Door lockset	2	
15-lb Roofing felt	850 sq. ft.		Awning-type aluminum windows	3	30" x 30"
Metal drip edge	112 lin. ft.		Sectional garage door	1	16' x 84"
Three-tab composite shingles	867 sq. ft.		Top door stop—garage door	17 lin. ft.	1x4
8" Horizontal vinyl siding	625 sq. ft.		Garage door facing	34 lin. ft.	1x4
Outside corner posts	4	3" x 1½" x 8'	Gutter system		
Starter strip	82 lin. ft.		Gutter	62 lin. ft.	
Window head flashing	3	36" piece	Drop outlets	4	
Window/door J-trim	36 lin. ft.		Downspouts	4	10' sections
Gable-end plywood panel siding	5	⅜" x 4 'x 8' (cut to fit)	Right end caps	2	
Soffits—12" ventilated	7	12' sections	Left end caps	2	
F-channel	116 lin. ft.		Gutter connectors	4	
Fascia—6" wide panels	116 lin. ft.		Gutter brackets	28	
Triangular attic vents (adjustable, with min. 1.87 sq. ft. net free ventilating area at each gable)	2		Downspout brackets	12	
Exterior door	1	36" x 80" prehung	Nails for installing:		
Interior door	1	32" x 80" prehung	Wall framing (tilt-up)	24 lbs.	16d
Double by-pass closet door	1	78" x 80" prehung	Trusses to top plate	½ lb.	10d
			Wall sheathing	12.2 lbs.	8d
			Roofing felt and drip edge	1 lb.	2d roofing nails
			Shingles	10.5 lbs.	3d roofing nails
			Vinyl siding	4 lbs.	4d roofing nails
			Gable-end plywood panels, molding	1 lb.	6d finish
			Paint and caulk		

¹ Size and quantity of forming lumber for concrete footings and slab depend on the footing depth and forming method.

Truss Types

There are many truss types, but the W-type and Howe trusses are the kinds most commonly used in garage construction. The truss chords and web members are constructed with 2x4s. The metal plate connectors have a number of spikes that are pressed into the wood at the joints to secure the members.

A roof truss contains a pair of rafters and the ceiling joist. When a truss is raised, the rafters and ceiling joist are installed as a single unit. The size and grade of lumber used, as well as the size of the connectors and the number of spikes it has, determine the strength of the truss. A truss built according to the engineered design will do the intended job.

ports such as girders, posts, or walls. Whether your two-car unit is the minimum width or 30 feet wide, a truss will make the span and the overhang at the eaves.

Installing Trusses

Frame the walls for a truss-roof structure the same as for stick framing, as discussed on pages 48 to 49. Then go on to build the roof, spacing the trusses 24 inches on center. Roof trusses arrive on the site in banded packages, which contain as few as 6 and as many as 12 or more. While a truss is rigid in upright position, it's flimsy in a flat position. You'll need three people—one at each end and one in the center—to handle the trusses and guard against excessive bending.

1 **Placing Trusses.** You can begin raising the trusses in the middle of the structure or at one end. Proper bracing is the key to safe installation. Mark each truss position

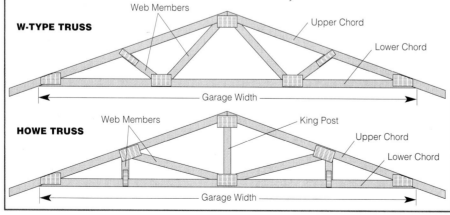

W-TYPE TRUSS — Web Members, Upper Chord, Lower Chord, Garage Width

HOWE TRUSS — Web Members, King Post, Upper Chord, Lower Chord, Garage Width

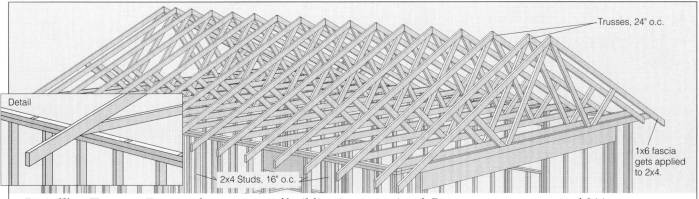

Detail

Trusses, 24" o.c.

1x6 fascia gets applied to 2x4.

2x4 Studs, 16" o.c.

Installing Trusses. Framing for a truss-roof building is conventional. Because trusses are spaced 24 in. o.c., every third stud in a 16-in.-o.c. wall will have a truss above it (inset).

on the top plate. Next, hand up the truss. Rest one end, peak down, in its position on the top plate. Move the other end to its position on the opposite wall. The first truss raised (rolled) is braced in position to the building with 2x4s. Scaffolding or catwalks are a big help when installing trusses. Make sure the truss is plumb and centered between the sidewalls.

2 **Fastening and Bracing.** Roll the truss into an upright position at the peak. Locate the truss on the layout mark, fasten it to the plate with two 10d nails on each side, and brace it. Metal tie-down anchors provide a more secure installation than toenailing and may be required by code. Check with your local building inspector.

Raise and fasten three trusses in position, ensuring each is centered between the bearing walls. Install spacer blocks between the trusses at the plates as you proceed. For 24-inch-on-center spacing, use 2x4 blocks 22½ inches long. Install same-length 2x4 blocks between the trusses at the peak to form the ridgeboard and ensure proper spacing at the top. The spacer blocks at the plate can be set vertically flush with the outside edge of the plate or as a frieze block, set square with the truss and extending out from the top plate. Spacer blocks with vents are available from the truss manufacturer. Install blocks with two 12d nails at each truss, face-nailing through the truss.

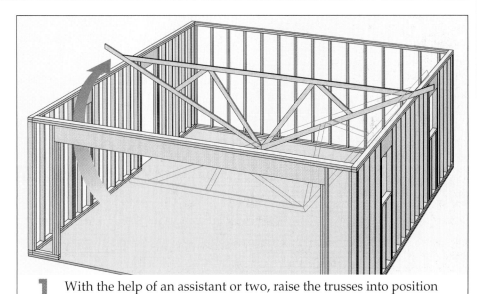

1 With the help of an assistant or two, raise the trusses into position on one wall, then the other.

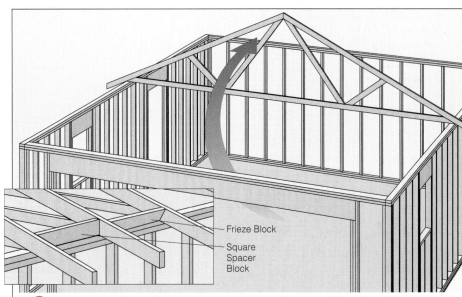

Frieze Block

Square Spacer Block

2 Once you have the truss in position, roll it upright and nail it in place. Install spacer blocks flush with the top plate or square with the truss as a frieze block.

3 **Installing the Braces.** With three trusses installed, nail a 12-foot or longer brace across the top, midway of the span on each side and over additional trusses as they are rolled into position. Also, run 1x4s in a V-shape at about a 45-degree angle from the plate to the peak on each side. Nail the diagonal to the underside of the truss top chord.

Gable-end trusses generally have 2x4 studs built into the component with the flat side flush with the truss edge. Align the outside edge of the bottom chord to the outside edge of the top plate and toenail to the top plate with 16d nails spaced 16 inches apart. This truss must line up vertically with the wall. Nail a long, straight 2x4 to the outside face of the stud wall with the end extended up near the center of the end truss and nail it to the truss near the peak. Leave the 2x4 brace in place until all the trusses are installed and braced, and the roof sheathing is nailed down. The diagonal braces nailed to the underside of the top chords can be left in place for greater stability of the roof.

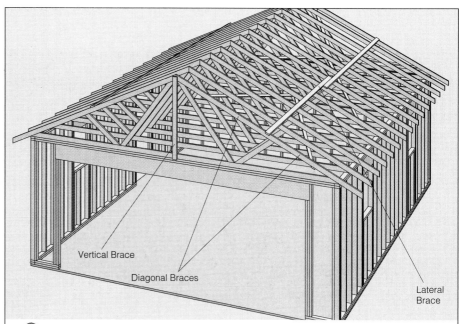

Vertical Brace

Diagonal Braces

Lateral Brace

3 Once you have three trusses installed, you can begin installing diagonal and lateral braces. The gable-end trusses get a vertical brace.

One-Car Detached Carport with Gable Roof

The one-car detached carport project shown here is partially enclosed and has a gable roof. This design encloses the rear wall of the unit for storage space, creating, in effect, a 5 x 12-foot storage shed. If you don't need the extra storage space, you'll build a detached carport that's open on all sides and supported entirely by posts. In this kind of carport the minimum dimensions are measured from roof edge to roof edge.

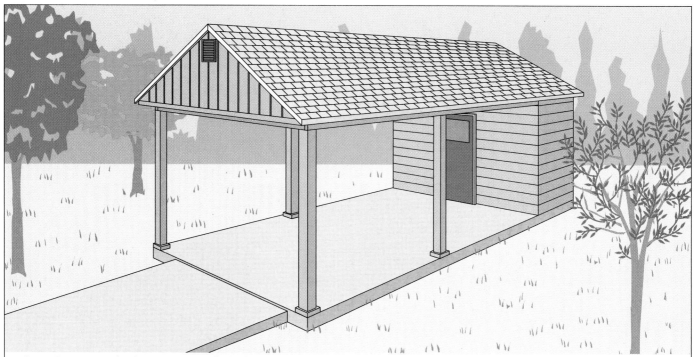

One-Car Detached Carport with Gable Roof. A storage area added to the back of an open carport is a good idea if you can afford the space in your yard.

Cutting & Materials List

NAME	QTY	SIZE
Foundation[1]		
Ready-mix concrete for footing (12" wide x 6" thick)	1 ½ cu. yd.	
Hollow-core concrete block for foundation wall, if required, per perimeter course	56	8" x 8" x 16"
Masonry cement (for 100 blocks)	1	70-lb. bag
Sand (for 100 blocks)	3 cu. ft.	
Gravel for 4" floor base	4 cu. yd.	
Sand for 1" min. cap on gravel	2 cu. yd.	
Polyethylene vapor barrier (6-mil)	312 sq. ft.	
Ready-mix concrete for 4-inch-thick floor slab	4 cu. yd.	
Anchor bolts	11	½" dia.
Concrete post-support piers	4	8" x 8" x 8"
Framing		
Sill plate gasket	33 lin. ft.	
Sill plate (pressure-treated)	2	12' 2x4s
	2	64" 2x4s
Bottom plate	2	12' 2x4s
	2	64" 2x4s
Studs (16" o.c.)		
Corner posts	12	8' 2x4s
Spacer blocks	12	12" 2x4s
King studs	4	8' 2x4s
Jamb studs	4	84" 2x4s
Wall studs	23	8' 2x4s
Window sill and cripple studs	1	12' 2x4 (cut to fit)
Gable-end	4	12' 2x4s (cut to fit)
Top plate	2	12' 2x4s
	1	12' 2x4 (cut to fit)
Top plate caps	2	12' 2x4s
	1	12' 2x4 (cut to fit)
Headers		
Window	2	35" 2x12s
36" Door	2	41" 2x6s
Support posts	4	8'6" 6x6s
Open-span header beams	4	20' 2x8s
	2	12' 2x8s
Ceiling joists (16" o.c.)	21	12' 2x6s
Rafters (16" o.c.)	44	9' 2x6s
Ridgeboard	2	14' 2x8s
Sway braces (uprights)	2	48" 2x4s
Sway braces (horizontals)	2	60" 2x4s
Sub-fascia (eaves)	4	14' 2x8s
Wall sheathing	9	½" x 4' x 9' plywood
Roof sheathing	18	½" x 4' x 8' plywood

NAME	QTY	SIZE
Roofing Siding, and Finish		
15-lb Roofing felt	500 sq. ft.	
Metal drip edge	96 lin. ft.	
Three-tab composite shingles	567 sq. ft.	
8" Horizontal vinyl siding	288 sq. ft.	
Outside corner posts	4	3" x 1½" x 8'
Starter strip	36 lin. ft.	
Window head flashing	1	32" piece
Window/door J-trim	12 lin. ft.	
Gable-end plywood panel siding	2	⅜" x 4' x 8' (cut to fit)
Gable-end batten	44 lin. ft.	
Gable-end horizontal trim board	2	14' 1x6s
Soffits—12" ventilated	5	12' sections
F-channel	56 lin. ft.	
Fascia board	92 lin. ft.	8" fir
Attic vents	2	18" x 12"
Soffit vents	4	8" x 12"
Exterior door	1	36" x 80" prehung
Door lockset	1	
Double-hung window	1	30" x 30"
Sash lock	1	
Gutter system		
Gutter	52 lin. ft.	
Drop outlets	4	
Elbows	12	
Downspouts	4	10' sections
Right end caps	2	
Left end caps	2	
Gutter connectors	4	
Gutter brackets	20	
Downspout brackets	12	
Nails for installing:		
Wall framing (tilt-up)	12 lbs.	16d
Ceiling joists to top plate and header	2 lbs.	8d
Rafters and bracing	1½ lbs.	8d
	5 lbs.	16d
Gable-end studs	1¼ lbs.	8d
Wall sheathing	5¼ lbs.	8d
Roof sheathing	10.5 lbs.	8d
Roofing felt and drip edge	1¼ lbs.	2d roofing nails
Shingles	7 lbs.	3d roofing nails
Vinyl siding	2 lbs.	4d roofing nails
Ceiling, gable-end plywood panels	½ lb.	6d finishing
Post-to-pier metal anchor straps	4	
Post-to-header metal anchor angles	8	
Paint and caulk		

[1] Size and quantity of forming lumber for concrete footings and slab depend on the footing depth and forming method.

Framing the Walls. After you've laid out and poured the foundation, begin construction of the unit by framing and tilting in place the walls of the storage room, following the steps on pages 41 to 43. If you need wider access to the storage area, say for a riding lawn mower, you can install prehung double exterior-type doors. Check the manufacturer's instructions for the rough opening requirements.

Once you've erected and braced the frame walls, set and temporarily brace the support posts for the carport proper. (See page 44.) Because the storage structure offers protection against racking, you don't need permanent bracing on the posts, though you may want to install it anyway as safety insurance.

Finishing the Structure. With the posts in place, install the double 2x8 header beams flush with the outsides of the posts. Support the ends of the double 2x8 headers at the storage walls on members of the corner posts cut to receive the header a minimum of 1½ inches. Now that you've erected the support structure, frame the roof, then sheathe the roof and frame walls. To make the structure weather-tight, shingle the roof and install the rear window and front door. Now you can cover the exterior walls with vinyl siding. Horizontal siding with an 8-inch exposure is specified for the walls, with plywood-and-batten siding for the gable ends, but you can use any siding you want. Install the trimwork, and your carport is ready for use.

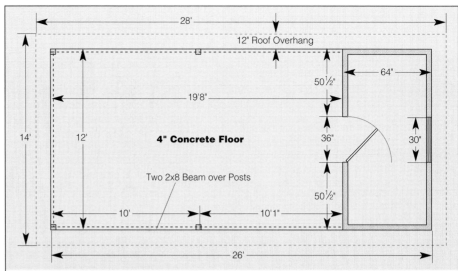

Framing the Walls. Start building the carport by raising the storage-area frame walls. Use the floorplan to determine opening locations.

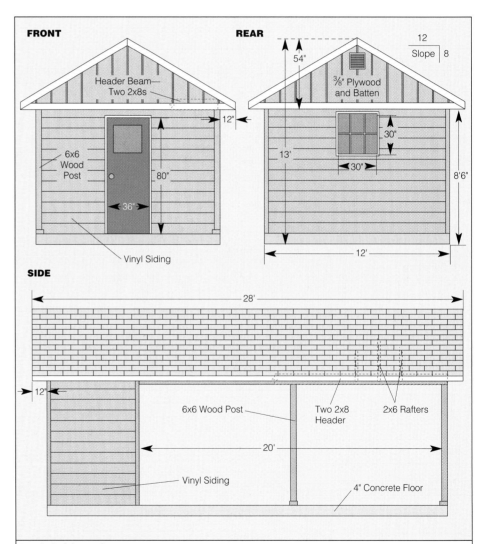

Finishing the Structure. Once you've erected the support structure, finish the carport with roofing and siding. Use any siding to suit your circumstances.

garage plans

How to Order Plans

(On pages 81 to 94.)

Our Exchange Policy

Blueprints are nonrefundable. However, should you find that the plan you have purchased does not fit your needs, you may exchange that plan for another plan in our collection within 60 days from the date of your original order. The entire content of your original order must be returned before an exchange will be processed. You will be charged a processing fee of 20% of the amount of the original order, the cost difference between the new plan set and the original plan set (if applicable), and all related shipping costs for the new plans. Contact our order department for more information. Please note: reproducible masters may only be exchanged if the package is unopened and CAD files cannot be exchanged and are nonrefundable.

Building Codes and Requirements

All plans offered for sale in this book and on our website (www.ultimateplans.com) are continually updated to meet the latest International Residential Code (IRC). Because building codes vary from area to area, some drawing modifications and/or the assistance of a professional designer or architect may be necessary to comply with your local codes or to accommodate specific building site conditions. We strongly advise you to consult with your local building official for information regarding codes governing your area.

Blueprint Price Schedule

Price Code	1 Set	5 Sets	Reproducible Masters	CAD	Materials List
AA	$60	$85	$125	$425	included
BB	$85	$105	$150	$450	included
CC	$110	$135	$175	$475	included
DD	$135	$155	$200	$500	included
EE	$150	$180	$230	$530	included
FF	$190	$220	$270	$570	included
A	$400	$440	$575	$1025	$85
B	$440	$525	$685	$1195	$85

Note: All prices subject to change.

Shipping & Handling

	1-4 Sets	5-7 Sets	Reproducibles	CAD
US Regular (7–10 business days)	$18	$20	$25	$25
US Priority (3–5 business days)	$25	$30	$35	$35
US Express (1–2 business days)	$40	$45	$50	$50
Canada Express (1–2 business days)	$80	$80	$80	$80
Worldwide Express (3–5 business days)	$100	$100	$100	$100

Note: All delivery times are from date the blueprint package is shipped (typically within 1-2 days of placing order).

Copyright Notice

All home plans sold through this publication are protected by copyright. Reproduction of these home plans, either in whole or in part, including any form and/or preparation of derivative works thereof, for any reason without prior written permission is strictly prohibited. The purchase of a set of home plans in no way transfers any copyright or other ownership interest in it to the buyer except for a limited license to use that set of home plans for the construction of one, and only one, dwelling unit. The purchase of additional sets of the home plans at a reduced price from the original set or as a part of a multiple-set package does not convey to the buyer a license to construct more than one dwelling.

Similarly, the purchase of reproducible home plans (sepias, mylars) carries the same copyright protection as mentioned above. It is generally allowed to make up to a maximum of 10 copies for the construction of a single dwelling only. To use any plans more than once, and to avoid any copyright license infringement, it is necessary to contact the plan designer to receive a release and license for any extended use. Whereas a purchaser of reproducible plans is granted a license to make copies, it should be noted that because blueprints are copyrighted, making photocopies from them is illegal.

Copyright and licensing of home plans for construction exist to protect all parties. Copyright respects and supports the intellectual property of the original architect or designer. Copyright law has been reinforced over the past few years. Willful infringement could cause settlements for statutory damages to $150,000.00 plus attorney fees, damages, and loss of profits.

Order Form

Please send me the following:

Plan Number: _____ (See plans.)

Price Code: _____ (See above.)

Basic Blueprint Package

	Cost
❏ CAD Files	$_____
❏ Reproducible Masters	$_____
❏ 1-Set Study Package	$_____
❏ 5-Set Package	$_____
❏ Additional plan sets:	
__ sets at $10.00 per set	$_____
❏ Print in mirror-reverse: $50.00 per order	$_____
*Please call all our order department or visit our website for availibility	
❏ Print in right-reading reverse: $150.00 per order	$_____
*Please call all our order department or visit our website for availibility	
Shipping (see chart above)	$_____
SUBTOTAL	$_____
Sales Tax (NJ residents add 7%)	$_____
TOTAL	$_____

Order Toll Free: 1-800-523-6789   By Fax: 201-760-2431
Creative Homeowner
24 Park Way
Upper Saddle River, NJ 07458

Name _____
(Please print or type)

Street _____
(Please do not use a P.O. Box)

City _____ State _____

Country _____ Zip _____

Daytime telephone ( ) _____

Fax ( ) _____
(Required for reproducible orders)

E-Mail _____

Payment ❏ Bank check/money order. No personal checks.
Make checks payable to Creative Homeowner

❏   ❏   ❏ American Express ❏

Credit card number _____

Expiration date (mm/yy) _____

Signature _____

SOURCE CODE **CA605**

1st Floor Plan

2nd Floor Plan

CH# 101152
Price Category: A

- This is a three-car garage plan featuring 838 sq. ft. of living space above.
- The craftsman styling is highlighted by stacked stone accents.
- In the efficient living quarters are a spacious family room, an eat-in kitchen, a bedroom with a wide closet and a bathroom.

1-Car Garage with Study

Plan #282801
Price code: AA

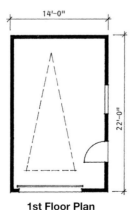

1st Floor Plan

- 308 sq. ft. of parking or storage space
- Great design for small building lots
- Size allows for ample wall-mounted storage
- Space-saving side entry door
- Complete materials list

2-Car Garage

CH# 451307
Price Category: CC

1st Floor Plan

- This two-car garage also features a workshop, perfect for those at-home projects.
- At 676 sq. ft., there is enough room for your cars and storage.
- The sleek and simplistic design will accentuate your existing home design.

All plans on pages 79–94 copyright by designer/architect

2-Car Garage with Apartment

1st Floor Plan

2nd Floor Plan

CH# 181684
Price Category: B

- This garage's living space incorporates features that you would not anticipate, such as the well-located fireplace.
- Enter this two-car garage through the foyer, and appreciate the integrated workshop/storage area downstairs.
- Upstairs, is a comfortable living space is created by the family room/dining room with fireplace, kitchen, laundry facilities, two bedrooms, and two shower rooms.

2-Car Carport with Apartment

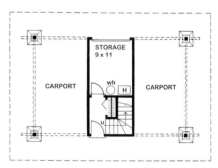

1st Floor Plan

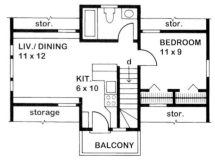

2nd Floor Plan

CH# 381041
Price Category: A

- The entryway to this garage space is centered between the two covered parking spaces.
- The overhangs on this design are decoratively trimmed, and its support pillars rest on striking, tapered stone columns.
- A winding stairway inside leads to a spacious one-bedroom apartment with a living/dining room, a bedroom, storage space, a kitchen, and a balcony.

All plans on pages 79–94 copyright by designer/architect

3-Car Garage with Apartment

24'-0"

WASHER/DRYER

3 CAR GARAGE
37'-4" x 23'-4"

38'-0"

1st Floor Plan

BATH
9'-6" x 5'-0"

CLOSET
11'-4" x 3'-0"

OPTIONAL
LAUNDRY
CHUTE

EAT-IN
KITCHEN
11'-4" x 13'-0"

FAMILY ROOM
14'-0" x 18'-0"

BEDROOM
11'-4" x 11'-8"

7' HIGH KNEE WALLS

2nd Floor Plan

CH# 101151
Price Category: A

- This is a three-car garage with a 750 sq. ft. studio above.
- With siding exterior reminiscent of a country barn, this plan would be perfect temporary quarters during construction of your permanent home, or it would be ideal for an in-law apartment, nanny quarters, college student apartment, etc.
- This design features an eat-in kitchen, a spacious family room, a bathroom and a bedroom with a roomy closet.

2-Garage with Workshop

CH# 631003
Price Category: FF

- This two-car garage offers plenty of car storage.
- Get all of your work done here, in the work area, office, and full bath.
- An additional storage area helps to keep things organized.

60'-0"

Stor.

Office
14-0x9-1

Garage
44-6x35-0
10' Ceiling

36'-0"

Work Area
14-0x20-0

16' x 8' door   16' x 8' door

1st Floor Plan

3-Car Garage

CH# 391084
Price Category: DD

- This spacious garage has plenty of room for your cars, and any additional storage.
- Three doors allow for a bit of privacy in some areas, while still allowing cars to come in and out of the space.
- Simple exterior design makes decorating easy.

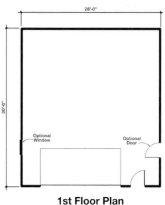

28'-0"

30'-0"

Optional
Window

Optional
Door

1st Floor Plan

All plans on pages 79–94 copyright by designer/architect

8 Garage Plans

3-Car Garage with Storage

1st Floor Plan

24'-0"
7,2 m

36'-4" X 22'-8"
10,90 X 6,80

38'-0"
11,4 m

33'-0" X 16'-0"
9,90 X 4,80

2nd Floor Plan

CH# 181188
Price Category: EE

- Three-car garage plan offers plentiful storage space for all of your needs.
- A second-floor storage area features a large area with beautiful windows, perfect for utilizing the space for work area.
- Two garage doors accommodate all different sizes of vehicles, perfect for flexibility when parking.

2-Car Garage with Storage

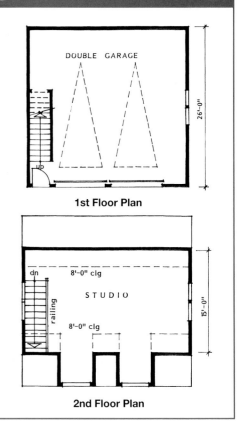

DOUBLE GARAGE

26'-0"

up

1st Floor Plan

dn   8'-0" clg

STUDIO

railing

8'-0" clg

15'-0"

2nd Floor Plan

Plan #282800
Price code: DD

- 676 sq. ft. of garage space
- Second floor can be used as storage or as a workshop or studio
- 8-ft.-high ceilings in studio
- Interior stairs to second floor
- Complete materials list

All plans on pages 79–94 copyright by designer/architect

2-Car Garage with Apartment

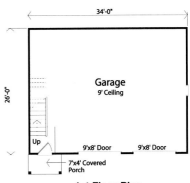

1st Floor Plan

34'-0"

26'-0"

Garage
9' Ceiling

Up

9'x8' Door   9'x8' Door

7'x4' Covered Porch

CH# 631004
Price Category: FF

- This garage is simple, yet efficient for your daily needs.
- The two-car garage space is perfect for your cars or for extra storage space.
- Upstairs, an apartment features a bedroom, bathroom, and kitchen.

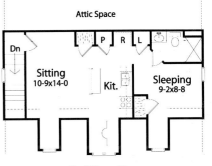

Attic Space

Dn

P R L

Sitting
10-9x14-0

Kit.

Sleeping
9-2x8-8

2nd Floor Plan

1-Car Garage

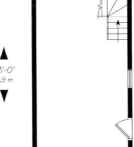

23'-0"
6.9 m

15'-0"
4.5 m

1st Floor Plan

CH# 181188
Price Category: EE

- One-car garage plan offers plentiful storage space for all of your needs.
- A second-floor storage area features a large area with beautiful windows, perfect for utilizing the space for work area.
- The garage door accommodates all different sizes of vehicles, perfect for flexibility when parking.

4-Car Garage

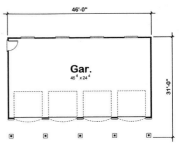

CH# 391592
Price Category: FF

- The exterior of this garage is accented by pillars, which separate each of the garage doors.
- Multiple garage doors allow for privacy in front of work or storage areas and flow where cars or other vehicles are stored.

46'-0"

Gar.
45'-4 x 24'-4

31'-0"

1st Floor Plan

All plans on pages 79–94 copyright by designer/architect

8 Garage Plans

2-Car Garage with Storage

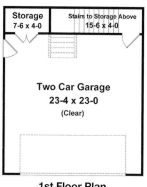

Storage
7-6 x 4-0

Stairs to Storage Above
15-6 x 4-0

Two Car Garage
23-4 x 23-0
(Clear)

1st Floor Plan

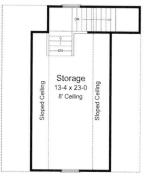

Sloped Ceiling

Storage
13-4 x 23-0
8' Ceiling

Sloped Ceiling

2nd Floor Plan

CH# 351073
Price Category: FF

- This garage plan offers a great layout, which provides for maximum flexibility.
- On the first floor, you'll enjoy the ample space provided for your two vehicles and also the separate storage area to keep your lawn equipment, tools, etc.
- The upstairs area includes an 8-ft. ceiling height in the middle portion of the space, which can be used for additional "attic overflow" and/or much needed work space.

2-Car Garage

Plan #282805
Price code: BB

- 768 sq. ft. of parking and storage space
- 8-foot overhang
- Parking areas separated by large center area
- Complete materials list

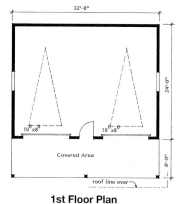

32'-0"

24'-0"

10'-0" x8'-0"   10'-0" x8'-0"

Covered Area

8'-0"

roof line over

1st Floor Plan

1-Car Garage

CH# 181176
Price Category: EE

- This one-car garage features a second level with 320 sq. ft. of storage space.
- Window shutters add a decorative element to the design.
- Simple design complements any house style.

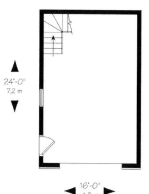

24'-0"
7,2 m

16'-0"
4,8 m

1st Floor Plan

All plans on pages 79–94 copyright by designer/architect

2-Car Garage with Apartment

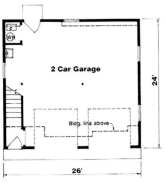

1st Floor Plan

2nd Floor Plan

CH# 471028
Price Category: EE

- Above the two-car garage is a spacious apartment, perfect for extra guests or live-in help.
- Upstairs, a well-equipped kitchen opens out to a living and dining area, with bedroom and bath nearby.
- The spacious garage area is perfect for cars or extra storage space.

2-Car Garage with Apartment

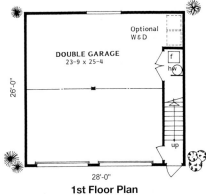

1st Floor Plan

2nd Floor Plan

Plan #282803
Price code: DD

- Enough space on the first floor for two cars as well as a washer and dryer, water heater, and furnace
- Enclosed stair to second floor
- Apartment includes living room, dining room, U-shaped kitchen, bath, and bedroom with a walk-in closet
- Complete materials list

2-Car Garage with Apartment

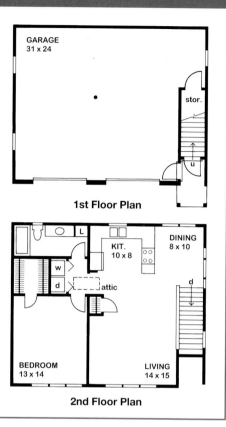

GARAGE
31 x 24

stor.

1st Floor Plan

L

KIT.
10 x 8

DINING
8 x 10

w

d

attic

d

BEDROOM
13 x 14

LIVING
14 x 15

2nd Floor Plan

CH# 381040
Price Category: A

- Oversized double-hung windows accentuate the exterior of this design, as does the first-floor brick facade.
- The covered entry provides access to both the two-car garage and second floor apartment.
- Upstairs, the apartment features a living room, dining area, kitchen, bathroom, bedroom, laundry closet, attic, and walk-in closet.

2-Car Garage with Storage

24'-0"

30'-4"

Garage
9' Ceiling

Up

9'x8' Door   9'x8' Door

1st Floor Plan

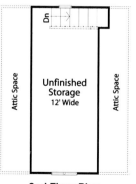

Dn

Attic Space

Unfinished
Storage
12' Wide

Attic Space

2nd Floor Plan

CH# 631005
Price Category: EE

- This spacious two-car garage has an unfinished loft for extra storage space.
- The floor plan is deep enough for boat and trailer storage.
- Two garage doors ensure ease of getting in and out of the garage but also provide privacy while working on projects.

All plans on pages 79–94 copyright by designer/architect

3-Car Garage with Apartment

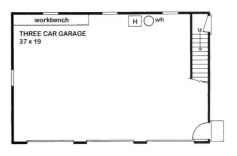

1st Floor Plan

2nd Floor Plan

CH# 381044
Price Category: A

- This garage features three garage doors, which are accentuated by glass panels along the top and flanked by traditional carriage lights.
- The main level provides space for three cars, along with a workbench.
- An interior stairway leads to the upstairs apartment, featuring a large bedroom with two closets, a living area, a bathroom illuminated by a skylight, and a kitchen/dining area.

3-Car Garage with Apartment

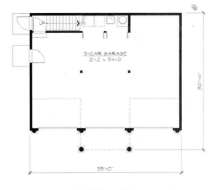

1st Floor Plan

2nd Floor Plan

CH# 551001
Price Category: A

- This three-car garage has a spacious interior, perfect for all of your needs.
- Columns separate the three garage doors, giving the garage a luxurious sense.
- Upstairs, an apartment features a deck, a living and dining area, a bedroom, a bathroom, and a kitchen.

All plans on pages 79–94 copyright by designer/architect

3-Car Garage with Apartment

1st Floor Plan

2nd Floor Plan

CH# 631006
Price Category: A

- Three cars can be comfortably parked inside this garage, with additional space for storage.
- Upstairs, an apartment features two bedrooms, a kitchen and breakfast room area, a family room, a washer and dryer, and a bathroom.
- This attractive design will go well in any neighborhood or with a variety of house styles.

3-Car RV Garage

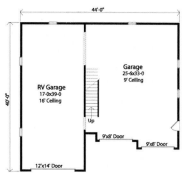

1st Floor Plan

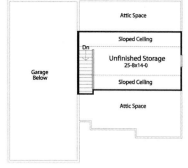

2nd Floor Plan

CH# 631007
Price Category: FF

- A stylish exterior adds curb appeal to this RV garage with attached two-car garage.
- Interior stairs lead to the second level loft, perfect for storage.
- The design of this garage is very flexible, perfect to suit your needs

All plans on pages 79–94 copyright by designer/architect

3-Car Garage

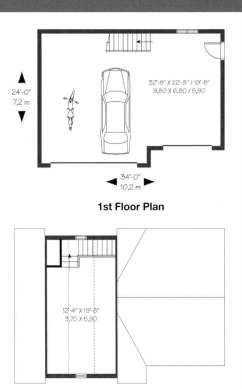

1st Floor Plan

32'-8" X 22'-8" / 19'-8"
9,80 X 6,80 / 5,90

24'-0"
7,2 m

34'-0"
10,2 m

12'-4" X 19'-8"
3,70 X 5,90

2nd Floor Plan

CH# 181189
Price Category: EE

- This three-car garage provides you with lots of flexible storage space, perfect for cars, bikes, etc.
- On the second level, there is an additional storage area of 295 sq. ft.
- Simple exterior design will not clash with preexisting architectural themes.

2-Car RV Garage

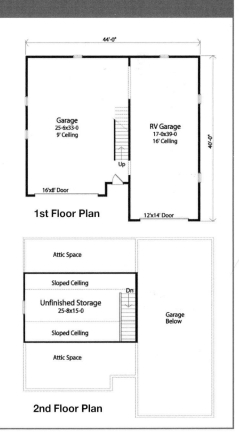

44'-0"

Garage
25-6x33-0
9' Ceiling

RV Garage
17-0x39-0
16' Ceiling

Up

16'x8' Door

12'x14' Door

40'-0"

1st Floor Plan

Attic Space

Sloped Ceiling

Unfinished Storage
25-8x15-0

Dn

Sloped Ceiling

Attic Space

Garage
Below

2nd Floor Plan

CH# 631008
Price Category: EE

- Front facing gables accent this RV garage with attached large garage for your car.
- This garage features plenty of storage space for all of your tools, equipment, and toys.
- Upstairs, a loft adds additional storage space, with both unfinished storage and attic space.

All plans on pages 79–94 copyright by designer/architect

8 Garage Plans

2-Car Garage with Apartment

1st Floor Plan

26'-0"
7,8 m

23'-0" X 24'-8"
6,90 X 7,40

28'-0"
8,4 m

18'-4" X 12'-4"
5,50 X 3,70

11'-8" X 12'-4"
3,50 X 3,70

2nd Floor Plan

CH# 181212
Price Category: FF

- The first level of this garage plan features room for two cars and a foyer.
- Upstairs, the living area includes a family room, kitchen, dinette, bedroom, and bathroom, perfect for in-laws, live-in help, or college students.
- The open parking area allows for multiple vehicles to be parked, or for part of the area to be used as additional storage space.

2-Car Garage with Apartment

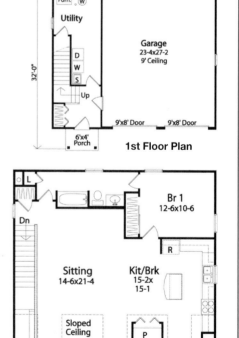

Furn. W

Utility

Garage
23-4x27-2
9' Ceiling

32'-0"

9'x8' Door   9'x8' Door

6'x4'
Porch

1st Floor Plan

L

Br 1
12-6x10-6

Dn

R

Sitting
14-6x21-4

Kit/Brk
15-2x
15-1

Sloped
Ceiling

P

2nd Floor Plan

CH# 631009
Price Category: B

- This garage plan provides the perfect guest suite, or can serve as a live-in worker's quarters.
- The two-car garage is designed with ample storage space, perfect for all of your tools and equipment when not in use.
- Upstairs, the apartment features an open floor plan with a kitchen and breakfast room area, sitting room, bedroom, and bathroom.

All plans on pages 79–94 copyright by designer/architect

2-Car Garage with Apartment

1st Floor Plan

2nd Floor Plan

CH# 631011
Price Category: A

- You'll have enough room for storage in this two-car garage.
- Upstairs is a one bedroom, one bathroom apartment with a galley kitchen, dining area, and open family and sitting areas.
- The traditional style of this garage apartment plan fits in easily with many different house and neighborhood styles.

2-Car Garage

Plan #282802
Price code: BB

- Option of one 16-ft. x 7-ft. garage door or two 9 ft. x 7-ft. doors
- 576 sq. ft. of parking and storage space
- Space-saving side entry
- Complete materials list

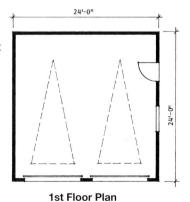

1st Floor Plan

3-Car Garage

Plan #282804
Price code: BB

- 768 square feet of parking and storage space
- Popular three-parking-bay design
- Combination of single-door and double-door entry
- Complete materials list

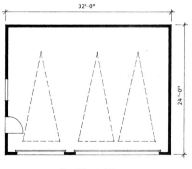

1st Floor Plan

All plans on pages 79–94 copyright by designer/architect

8 Garage Plans

2-Car Garage with Apartment

1st Floor Plan

2nd Floor Plan

CH# 181213
Price Category: B

- This plan combines a garage, storage space, and living space into an attractive and useful combination.
- On the first level, the two-car garage is joined by storage space, a half-bath, and a foyer entry.
- Upstairs, the living area features a family room, an eat-in kitchen, a laundry area, two bedrooms, and a shower room.

3-Car Garage with Apartment

1st Floor Plan

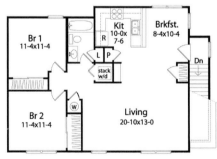

2nd Floor Plan

CH# 631013
Price Category: A

- When built with a permanent residence, this garage plan is perfect for the live-in worker's residence or for use as a guest suite.
- The three-car garage has direct access to the interior stairs leading to the upper level apartment.
- Upstairs, the spacious living area offers flexibility, with its two bedrooms, bathroom, open living area, kitchen, washer and dryer, and breakfast room.

All plans on pages 79–94 copyright by designer/architect

glossary

Anchor bolts Bolts set in concrete that fasten sills, columns, or beams to the foundation.

Batter boards Temporary structures that hold strings used to locate and square the corners of a building.

Bird's-mouth cut A cutout in a rafter where it crosses the top plate of the wall, providing a bearing surface for nailing. Also called a heel cut.

Box cornice A cornice completely closed with trimwork.

Brace Framing member used to strengthen a part of the structure.

Butt joint Lumber pieces joined at the ends.

Cat's paw Variation on a pry bar that removes deep-set nails mistakenly driven into framing lumber.

Common rafter Rafter that extends from the top plate to the ridge.

Control joints Indentations set into concrete to prevent cracking.

Cornic Molding where the rafter ends meet the eaves.

Cripple stud Short stud used as support in wall openings.

Drip edge The metal or vinyl projection along the eaves or rakes of a roof that allows water to run off or drip away from the underlying construction.

Fascia Wood trim applied to rafter tails at eaves or to end rafters on the gable end of a building.

Flashing A metal sheet used at breaks in a roof wherever water might leak in.

Footing A widened, below-ground base of a foundation wall, or a poured-concrete base on which precast concrete piers are placed.

Gable roof Roof with two flat, sloping sides that meet at a ridgeboard.

Hurricane ties Metal fasteners used to secure rafters in structures subject to hurricane winds.

Jack stud A partial stud nailed next to full studs to support the header at door openings. Also called a trimmer.

Joist A structural member placed perpendicular to beams in floor framing.

Joist hanger A metal anchor used to support a joist framed into a header or beam. Also called a joist clip.

King stud Regular length studs to which header members are attached. May or may not be located at on-center positions.

Lag screw Large hex-head screw used for fastening wood framing pieces.

Ledger The wood or metal member attached to a beam, studding, or a wall to support joist or rafter ends.

Monolithic concrete pour foundation One that is accomplished without using construction joints, or separation. The footing and foundation are poured as a single component, eliminating a lot of formwork.

Mudsill A wood foundation member bolted to a concrete slab or foundation and on which other framing members can be placed; mudsills are usually pressure-treated 2x4s or 2x6s.

OSB (oriented-strand board) Panel material made from strands of wood oriented in one direction and compressed under high pressure.

Panel clip Metal device for joining two edges of plywood together.

Pier block A concrete block used to support foundation members such as posts, beams, girders, or joists.

Plate Horizontal support member in a frame wall, such as a top, bottom, or sill plate.

Post anchor Metal fastener used for joining wood posts to concrete piers.

Post cap Metal fastener used for joining posts to beams.

Pry bar Flat bar available in a variety of sizes from 8 to 18 inches with a notch for removing stubborn nails.

Rafter Wood or metal support piece on a sloping roof.

Rafter tail The portion of a rafter that extends past the building to form the eaves.

Ridgeboard Horizontal support at the ridge of a roof to which opposing rafters are attached.

Ridgeboard splice For a long ridge-board span, an angle splice that must be cut into the support to create a stronger butt joint.

Ridge cut End cut on a rafter that fits it to the ridgeboard.

Roll roofing Asphalt roofing that comes in rolls 36 inches wide, 36 feet long. The roofing is rolled out and may be mopped down with tar.

Roof pitch Angle of the roof sides expressed in a ratio of span to rise.

Roofing felt An asphalt underlayment required under asphalt shingles.

Screeding Leveling of concrete flatwork.

Shakes Wooden shingles hand-split from a timber.

Sheathing Panels that lie between the studs and siding of a structure.

Shed roof Also called a pitched flat roof, this design carries a larger snow load and may require sturdier framing.

Shim An often tapered piece of wood used to level and secure a structure.

Soffit An underside area of a framing member or building part.

Starter strip A strip at the bottom of the outside wall, between the sheathing and the siding.

Stud Vertical member of a frame wall, placed at both ends and usually every 16 or 24 inches on center. Provides structural framing and facilitates covering with sheathing and drywall or paneling.

Troweling Finishing the concrete after it has been screeded.

Truss Manufactured roof-support member internally supported through cross braces called webs. W-type and Howe trusses are the most common ones used in garage construction.

Turnaround Space permitting, an area for cars to park and turn around without having to back into the street.

index